How To WRITE THE RIGHT BOOK FAST

HOW TO WRITE THE RIGHT BOOK FAST
Position Yourself As An Authority, Attract Qualified Leads, Build Your Brand, and Increase Your Income in 90 Days or Less.

©2017 Trevor Crane

All Rights Reserved. Printed in the U.S.A.

ISBN-13: 978-1976178375
ISBN-10: 1976178371

All rights reserved. This book or any portion thereof may not be reproduced or used in any manner whatsoever without the express written permission of the publisher except by a reviewer, who may quote brief passages and/or show brief video clips in a review.

Disclaimer: The Publisher and the Author make no representation or warranties with respect to the accuracy or completeness of the contents of this work and specifically disclaim all warranties of fitness for a particular purpose. No warranty may be created or extended by sales or promotional materials. The advice and strategies contained herein may not be suitable for every situation. This work is sold with the understanding that the Publisher is not engaged in rendering legal, accounting or other professional services. If professional assistance is required, the services of a competent professional person should be sought. Neither the Publisher nor the Author shall be liable for damages arising therefrom. The fact that an organization or website is referred to in this work as citation and/or potential source of further information does not mean that the Author or the Publisher endorses the information, the organization or website may provide or recommendations it may make. Further, readers should be aware that internet websites listed in this work may have changed or disappeared between when this work was written and when it is read.

Publishing and Design:

Ordering Information: Quantity sales. Special discounts are available on quantity purchases by corporations, associations, and others. For details, contact the publisher at the address above. Orders by U.S. trade bookstores and wholesalers.

Please contact: 800-273-1625 | support@trevorcrane.com | EpicAuthor.com

First Edition

For more information about Trevor Crane or to book him for your next event or media interview, please visit: TrevorCrane.com/media

TREVOR CRANE

How To
WRITE
THE
RIGHT
BOOK
FAST

Position Yourself As An *Authority*, Attract *Qualified Leads*, Build Your Brand, and *Increase Your Income* …effortlessly.

DOWNLOAD THIS AUDIO FOR FREE

JUST GO TO:
TrevorCrane.com/freeaudio

FREE TRAINING TO BECOME AN AUTHOR

Make this the year you "finally" write your book!

Becoming a published is the most powerful way to grow your business, your brand, your mission and your legacy.
—**Trevor Crane**

FREE TRAINING
EpicAuthor.com/free

YOUR BOOK IS ONLY THE BEGINNING

Within the first 12 months after publishing my first book, my wife and I 10x'd our business.

I had no idea how powerful a book could be.

The success we experienced was so explosive, it was like throwing a bucket of gasoline on a campfire.

Writing a book to grow your business is the most <u>powerful</u> and <u>impactful</u> thing you can do to forward your business, cause, mission or legacy.

*Our bestselling author family.

"This program is a no-brainer for speakers and entrepreneurs who want to impress prospects and command higher fees. Here's what happened in less than 24 hours: My book became a #1 bestseller in 4 countries. It opened up a series of hot conversations with very tough-to-get-to folks. I made 18 new-sales of a brand new on-line program. I was invited to write a column for 2 major publications. And, I've already gotten invitations from major print and TV Media."
—Jess Todtfeld, #1 Bestselling Author and Founder of Success In Media, Inc.

"I put off getting my book done for years. But finishing it and hugging #1 helped me close over $25K from my first 90-minute talk as a bestsellers author. My credibility was through the roof. Shortly after, I launched a one-day earn with only 12 people, and closed $45K of new business in just one day! Can't wait to write the next one!"
—Robyn Crane, #1 Bestselling Author and Creator of the FEMM Movement

"The best thing about my book is how much easier it's made it for me to help more people. It was a simple step-by-step system and more importantly the process didn't take away from my business, or my family time. I also wrote a better book with Trevor's guidance. After 2 years of feeling like I wasn't getting anywhere will my book, Trevor made it easy. I can't thank him enough, and for helping me leverage this into my $100K-/month business."
—Steve Napolitan, #1 Bestselling Author and Founder of Client Capture Course

"All I can say is BAM!!! 6-Weeks ago, my book was an idea. Today, it's a #1 International Bestseller! BEFORE it was even written, it helped me book a talk, and presell 250 copies. I've got new speaking gigs around the globe, and I've launched my fits online program that's being fed by my book. I'm freaking thrilled!"
—Bronkar Lee, #1 Bestselling Author and Motivational Speaker

CONTENTS

Book Bonuses iv
Dedication xi
INTRO 1
    Impact And Income 3
PREPARE 29
    1   Get Clarity 31
    2   Set Yourself Up To Win 45
    3   Tell The World 55
PLAN 69
    4   Strategy 71
    5   Structure & Story 93
    6   Set A Date 145
PRODUCE 151
    7   Speak, Scribe, Source 153
    8   Build Your Publishing Team 173
PUBLISH 181
    9   Self-Publishing Vs. Traditional Publishing 183
    10   Pre-Launch 193
    11   7 Phases Of Your Epic Book Launch 205
PROFIT 219
    12   Promotion With A Launch Team 221
    13   Big Money With Your Book 233
THE END? 246
BIG MONEY PROGRAMS 249
    I   Free Training 250
    II   Epic Author Academy 251
    III Epic Author Mentoring 252
About The Author 255
More Books By Trevor Crane 260
Acknowledgements 263

To my mom and dad.
You always loved me and believed in me.
What more could a kid ask for?
(A lot apparently. Sorry for being a pain in the ass.)

You Are Powerful Beyond Measure

"Our deepest fear is not that we are inadequate.
Our deepest fear is that we are powerful beyond measure.
It is our light not our darkness that most frightens us.
Your playing small does not serve the world;
There is nothing enlightened about shrinking so that other people
won't feel insecure around you.
We were all meant to shine as children do.
It is not just in some of us, it is in everyone.
And as we let our own light shine,
we unconsciously give other people permission to do the same.
As we are liberated from our own fear,
our Presence automatically liberates others."
—Marianne Williamson

INTRO

"If you can dream it, you can do it."
—Walt Disney

INTRO
Impact and Income

"The significant problems we face cannot be solved at the same level of thinking we were at when we created them."
—**Albert Einstein**

Meet Jamie

Jamie is changing the world.

Her mission is to help children with severe autistic challenges, and their parents.

Why does this matter to Jamie? Why does she wake up every morning with a burning passion to make a difference? Because of her son, Dominic.

At two years old, within 90 minutes of receiving his routine vaccinations, Dominic developed a 105 fever and started convulsing with seizures. Jamie rushed him back to the ER. The doctors assured her that this was a rare reaction and he'd be fine. But Dominic wasn't fine.

He dissipated from being a happy, healthy, talking boy to being chronically sick and losing his ability to speak. He became a hair pulling, screaming, fecal smearing, insomniac with grand mal seizures. The doctors told Jamie that, because of his viral encephalitis, his chances of survival past the age of 22 is only 50 percent.

Doctors said he'd never talk again. They told Jamie that not only does he not have the capacity to communicate, but also, he didn't have the mental ability to understand anymore. Never again would she hear her son say, "MOMMY."

Dominic's symptoms were eventually diagnosed as non-verbal autistic.

But Jamie couldn't accept that diagnosis. Jamie Juarez Melillo, is a scientist, currently getting her doctorate at The University Of Southern California (USC), dedicated her life to finding something that could help.

What she wanted more than anything, was to have her baby boy back. She refused to accept that he couldn't understand, or that he wouldn't talk to her ever again.

After tireless years of research and study, Jamie developed a revolutionary protocol that has enabled her son to communicate. Jamie gave Dominic a way to say, "MOMMY" again and now she wants to share her process with others.

Jamie's desire is to speak around the world, training and educating therapists and parents to use her system to help their non-verbal autistic kids communicate.

When Jamie first approached me about her book, I got excited. Nothing lights me up more, than to work with people with a vision and a cause that makes a difference.

When she told me she had most of her book written already, I got even more excited, because I knew how fast things could grow for her.

But Jamie was having some challenges.

When she shared her writing with people, she discovered that her message wasn't getting through. The results and praise that she was hoping for, didn't come.

Based on this feedback, Jamie began to realize that maybe her book was not effectively communicating with people.

Jamie confided in me, that she thought she may have written the *wrong* book.

When I reviewed what she had written, I immediately saw the challenge.

While the book seemed to have very good content, the problem was that it read more like a complicated science book, than a book geared toward a parent with a child, who needed Jamie's help.

When I discussed this with Jamie, I asked her who she was writing this book for. Who do you want to read this book?

Jamie's answer was, "everybody."

Do you see the conflict yet?

Let me explain.

Recently I spoke with a Dr. David Sperbeck, a pediatric neuropsychologist who does about 600 neuro-psych evaluations a year, for close to 35 years. His specialty is working with ADHD, executive functioning disorders, working memory disorders, and writing and reading disorders.

He said that back when he was doing psychotherapy he would have his patients write out everything they had talked about in the previous session.

They would come back to him for the next session and he'd say, "Okay, let me see your notes from last week." Looking at it, he often found writing not only unrecognizable from their conversation, but in some ways it was indecipherable. He was confused. He'd asked them to write out *exactly* what they thought he was saying.

What Dr. Sperbeck discovered was, what he was _transmitting_ was not what was being _received_. He further acknowledged, that it wasn't as much their fault as it was his. He said to me simply, "I just wasn't communicating in a way that they could relate to."

Back to Jamie.

In Jamie's example, by trying to appeal to everyone, the families, the doctors, the government, the media and therapists working with these types of children… Jamie wasn't connecting with anyone.

Who you choose to write your book for, will greatly determine the *content* that goes in your book.

Now, had the purpose of Jamie's book just for the scientific community, perhaps it would have been okay.

The truth is, since Jamie wasn't clear about her perfect audience from the beginning, and she didn't clearly understand the precise purpose of her book, she added content that wasn't relevant and ultimately distracting.

Fortunately, this is fixable.

After Jamie and I had a brief conversation, Jamie got clarity about her real purpose. Jamie is passionate about helping the parents and therapists of children with severe autism.

Her audience isn't the whole world. It's the moms and dads who have to deal with these challenges on a daily basis.

Without this clarity, Jamie believes that her message would have fallen on deaf ears, and few, if any people would ever learn about her book, her program, and how she can support them.

Now, truth be told, Jamie is <u>not</u> an anomaly in this sense. In fact, I find this pattern to be the norm. Now that I have a publishing company, focused on helping people write books, and turn them into their most powerful marketing tool, I see this challenge nearly every single day.

I think of books like this, as a buried treasure—*without a map.*

Without knowing who she was *targeting,* who she was *talking* to, and without having a <u>clear message</u> and <u>call to action,</u> Jamie would have been disappointed with her book.

<u>Meet Steve</u>

I first met Steve years ago when my wife and I were first dating. He was attending an event where he was learning to improve as a professional speaker, and how to grow his coaching and consulting business.

Steve and I hit it off immediately.

In the years that followed we stayed in touch and I got to see Steve win, and sometimes lose, in his business.

About 5 years ago, Steve started talking about how he knew hey *should* have a book, and he knew how *powerful* it could be to grow his business.

2 years went by—no book.

After 3 years, Steve reached out to me again saying he'd finally "started" his book.

Near the end of 2015, Steve reached out to me again and said he'd had enough. His book still wasn't done, and he needed my help.

However, while he knew writing a book done was important, he was still *conflicted*.

Steve said his main concern was <u>time</u>.

Since he so busy working in his business, and trying to be successful, he didn't think he had the *time* to get his book done.

He also didn't want to sacrifice his *family time*.

Steve realized in his previous business that he had unknowingly turned into a work-a-holic, much like his father had been, when he was growing up.

Steve vowed to never do that to his family again.

Steve had also been going through a challenging time in is career.

After a failed business venture, in which Steve moved his entire family from San Francisco to Australia, and then back again, Steve was staring over *from zero.*

But after seeing the successes my wife and I had with our newly published books, he said he couldn't wait any longer.

According to Steve, he was, "extremely frustrated" that he'd not yet gotten it done, even though he'd been thinking about it and talking about it for years.

What did Steve hope a book could give him?

More <u>speaking gigs</u>. More <u>clients</u>. And more <u>money</u>.

He also wanted better <u>branding</u> and <u>marketing</u> so he could not only book more talks, but increase his fees, and make more sales on the back-end of his presentations.

He wasn't really sure how a book could help him do all of that. And, that's why he asked for my help.

However, as I said, early on in our conversation, Steve kept-on about how *busy* he was, and how he didn't have the extra time it would take to write his book.

This is one of the "myths" floating around out there that hold people back:

MYTH:
It takes a lot of time to write a book.
(At least a good book.)

I assured Steve, that if he was coachable, and used my system step-by-step, that he'd most likely get his book done in less than 24 hours.

He said, "24 hours? You've got to be kidding me… HOW is that possible?"

I replied, "Trust me."

So he did. And we got started. Once we got *clarity*, and created a *plan* for Steve, one that didn't just include *writing* his book, but also how to launch a powerful *marketing plan*, at the same time… Steve not only became a #1 international bestselling author, in less than 24 hours, he also added new clients to his business BEFORE his book was even completed.

One of my favorite stories Steve shared with me is when he had someone send him a $5,000 check in the mail with a note that just said, "Steve I want to hire you. I don't have time now, but here's a check, just to let you know I'm serious. I know you're going to be really busy with new clients, now that you have your book coming out, and I wanted to make sure I was on your calendar."

And… Steve did get his book done—FAST.

It was funny, at one point in the process, Steve called me up, concerned that we weren't doing enough work, and that he wasn't going to meet his deadline.

Here's a text he sent me the other day, after we finished his book.

> *"Brother, I want to thank you. For me the biggest part was that you made it so simple and step-by-step. Remember, I even called you and said, 'Trev, I don't feel I'm doing enough! How are we going to get everything done, and still hit our deadlines?!' And you said, 'Steve, did you do your homework this week?' And I said 'yes.' Then you said 'Okay, great. You're done for the week then. Go be with your family.'*
>
> *Trevor, I'm still blown-away that we finished on time, and most importantly, that it didn't take away from my business, or my family time. You're the man."*

(Sure I could have left out the "You're the man part," but I like it!

Later in the book, I'll share with you *how* he did it.

For now, I just want you to know that there is a RIGHT book for you, and that you can write it FAST.

But the hard truth is, even though nearly everyone WANTS to write a book, less than 1% actually DO.

Why?

Typically just one thing: *Clarity*.

Without clarity, most people are overwhelmed. People need a SYSTEM to follow, that bypasses the pitfalls, and avoids the hurdles. Just like Dorothy from the Wizard Of Oz, you need a clear path that leads you down the yellow-brick road towards Emerald City of "authorship."

…Without that path, they get lost in the woods, scared of the lions and tigers and bears, and they waste precious time, and they get frustrated, and unfortunately get carried off by flying monkeys—and never get their book done.

Or, worse, they do get their book done, only to find out it stinks. Or they wrote it for the wrong audience or about the wrong subject, or they just plain don't know how to leverage it into what they ultimately want.

Subsequently:

- 12 months from now, their book still isn't finished.
- They realize they've wasted hundreds of hours.
- They're more frustrated than ever.
- Most just give up.

So if you've ever felt:

Frustrated that you aren't already growing your business with your book, or you're *wasting time and money* on things that have resulted in little or no return for your efforts. Or, if you've ever felt under appreciated, or undervalued… or if you're simply *pissed off* at not getting your book done already…

You are not alone.

In this book, I'll share with you the exact steps I took to write, publish, and launch 10 bestselling books, how my 9-year old daughter has 9 bestselling books, and numbers examples of how my clients and I are leveraging those books to make a difference, and rapidly grow our businesses and expand our impact.

<u>Imagine for a moment...</u>

What if you started writing your book today. And you KNEW, beyond a doubt, that you had a proven SYSTEM in place to make sure you write the RIGHT book, and that you'd finish it, and LAUNCH it... in as little as 3 months?

What if I told you you could be a bestselling author as well?

And if you knew with perfect CLARITY what you needed to do each <u>day</u>, each <u>week</u>, and each <u>month,</u> to make writing your new bestseller a reality...

How cool would that be?

Just imagine, instead of handing out a business card at the next conference or networking event you attend... you had a beautiful copy of your book, a book that you were proud of. A book that you knew with confidence, would help people and if you placed it in the right hands, would ultimately want more of you, your products and your services.

Your book is your most powerful marketing tool.

There is literally no other device that establishes as much instant authority, and builds as much credibility, trust and desire for you, your products and your services.

Once You Become An Author:

- Instead of *chasing* clients, you can have them coming to you.
- Instead of *convincing* people, you spend time helping people.
- Instead of *"trying"* to position yourself as an *"expert"*, you already are the expert.
- Instead of trying to *"prove"* yourself to your prospects, you get to "pick" the best clients that you WANT to work with.
- Instead of *"discounting"* your fees, you can INCREASE your prices, and the VALUE you bring your clients, and set yourself apart from the competition.
- You can also get more media, speaking engagements, more leads, better clients, make a difference, feel more fulfilled and change the world.

A book… the "right" book… YOUR book… can change everything.

Now, let me clear-up one myth right now.

MYTH: You have to be a great writer to be an author.

Contrary to common belief, you don't need to be a great writer to have a phenomenal book.

You don't need to spend *months on end* in some cabin in the woods writing.

In fact, you don't even need to have a *finished* book to *gain more clients*.

That's right.

You can start gaining more leads, and earning more money <u>while</u> you create your book.

I'll show you how soon.

What you will learn in this book will *dissolve* all your fears of getting it wrong again, having your business and brand look bad, and wasting any more time on things that *don't* work.

You don't have to *guess*.
It's more like a scientific formula.

It's called the *Epic Author System*.

By following the proven process I share with you in this book, you will have a book that virtually guarantees you will:

- Get media *attention*,
- Create a system to get *consistent leads*,
- Build a burning desire for people to *want to buy from you*, and
- Grow your *business*.

I'll also show you how you can use a book to get to hard to reach CEO's and influential people, and how to easily get past the *closed doors* of your prospects who are being bombarded by traditional noise and marketing.

I'll share with you a simple strategy, that you can use when you interact with your client, so you and your business will be *remembered*—in a good way.

When you have the *right* book, your customers' skepticisms about you and your business will quickly dissolve.

You will be empowered to *charge higher fees*.

You and your brand will become *sought after, recognized*, and *respected*.

More importantly, *you* will be responsible for the positive impact you have on your customers; locally, internationally…

You choose.

Imagine having your ideal target audience seeing you as having:

Authority, Credibility, Expertise …and even *Celebrity*.

What could it mean to you, if you had the RIGHT BOOK, that created immediate trust, and ignited their desire to want more of you and what you do?

Does it sound too good to be true?

Well it's a *reality* for many authors who know the secrets and the strategies.

I hope you're ready.

Who Am I to Help You?

You might be thinking, "Trevor, who are you to say all this?"

I'm glad you asked.

I'm the son of a horse-shoer, or "farrier" if you want to know the right lingo. I grew up in Phoenix, Arizona.

I am the oldest of 3 kids. (I have 2 sisters.)

My parents were divorced 5 times. I had 2 different fathers, and 5 different step mothers. At one point, I had 8 different step brothers and step sisters, and my family struggled to put food on the table and pay the bills.

At about 7 years old, I found out that my great, great, grandfather had been rich. Super, duper wealthy. Apparently, long before I was born, our family had been worth millions.

I looked around and wondered what the hell happened?

Where did all that money go. <u>We sure didn't have any</u>. *Our family motto was, "We can't afford it."* Money was often at the core of what my parents fought about.

As a kid, I was *embarrassed* because my mom had to make my clothes.

Today, I'm embarrassed that I was such an ungrateful little jerk, and that I didn't better appreciate what my parents had to do, to take care of us. And how unappreciative I was about what we did have.

My step dad was a roofer. The only thing worse than his farts, were his beer-smelling burps. He didn't like me much.

When I was in high school, I can still feel the pain of him yelling at my mom about what a *"worthless little mother fucking son of a bitch,"* I was.

Now… I'm NOT sharing this because I want your sympathy. I don't need it.

MANY people had it much harder than I did.

And my challenges helped to sculpt me into who I am today. I wouldn't trade my history for yours, or anybody's background.

And my parents really gave me the only 2 things I think that are REALLY important.

1. Unconditional love, and

2. They believed in me.

One of the greatest gifts they gave me, (my real mom and dad, not all the step parents) was the belief that I could do anything. In that regard, I was the luckiest kid in the world.

The ONLY reason I share any of this "poor kid" story with you, is to let you know where I came from. We didn't have money. We didn't have what I thought "success" was.

But, I did grow up with the knowing that, "someone" in my family, "had" in the past, "made it." I wanted that too.

And since my parents brainwashed me into thinking I could do anything. I believed them.

When I was 7 years old, I decided I'd figure out how to "rebuild" the family fortune.

Eventually, I decided the best way to do that was to own my own business.

Years later, when I was earning millions, I thought I was finally on my way to fulfilling that childhood dream. Until I lost everything. Boo.

But then, I built it back. Yay!

And then, just because one time wasn't enough, I lost everything again. Boo.

The second time, was definitely the most painful.

In 2009, I filed a 2.2million dollar bankruptcy.

I lost all my stuff, including my money, houses, cars, etc. But I also lost a woman I was in love with at the time, who took our 2-year old daughter away, and left the state.

I even had to give my dog away to a friend, because I didn't have a place to live.

At that time, my self worth and net worth were so intertwined, that when I lost one, I lost the other. I felt worthless, useless and hopeless. And, I was homeless.

Now, I didn't have to sleep on the street or abandoned buildings. Thank God, I had friends who loved me enough to let me stay with them.

But I share all of this with you, because I want you to know that I hit bottom. And that perhaps, if I share my story, you might be more likely to overcome any challenges that you're going through to be successful

Through it all, I knew that was somehow these "setbacks,» had to be "setups" for my eventual success, but at times it was very hard to keep the faith.

I also felt like,

No one would ever trust me again.

When I found out where my daughter's mother decided to live, I bought a one-way ticket to New York City (NYC) to be near my now 3-year-old daughter.

I also had to rebuild my business and my life. A friend was kind enough to let me move into his basement.

During my first winter in NYC, since I didn't have enough money for the subway, I carried my 3-year-old daughter on my shoulders, all over the city. It was freezing cold. All I had to wear were my torn jeans, and a flimsy denim jacket I borrowed from a friend.

Without a place to live of my own, I even had to give my dog Mojo away.

Ashamed, I did my best to never let my daughter see my struggles or my embarrassment.

One of the hardest parts of it all was the feeling that no one would ever trust me again, because I felt like,

A Loser

In that state, it felt like I had *no value* to offer to another human being. I definitely didn't think about being an author, or that anyone would ever want to read one of my books.

I wouldn't wish an experience like this on my worst enemy.

I made a series of poor decisions.

I refused to accept the help and mentoring of others. I was stubborn. I thought I knew it all, and I kept thinking that I was smart enough to figure it all by myself.

I blamed other people for my problems. I started fights. I tried to sue the people who had "wronged" me. All without really looking in the mirror, and facing the truth, about the guy who was *ultimately responsible* for my actions. What a joke.

But finally, I started getting it right.

I stopped blaming others. I accepted that I had actually been the cause of all of my problems, and the great thing about that was, while I couldn't control other people, I could take charge of myself.

Over several years, I rebuilt my business and my life.

I sought out new mentors. I found the fortitude to push through challenges, or better yet, I got insight from people smarter than I was, so I could avoid them in the first place.

And, while it worked. It wasn't great.

I was very busy putting in a lot of effort, for little return. But when I *finally* became an author, everything changed.

Instantly, my positioning shifted. The trust and authority I was trying to push down peoples throats, was now nearly automatic. I stopped having to work hard to convince people to work with me.

Instead, people were *attracted* to work with me.

I think the difference was a confluence of combination of things. It was definitely the book and becoming an author, but it was also my mindset. It was especially the mentors I had around me helping me. And most certainly it was about how I spent my time, and the MAP's (Massive Action Plans) that my new circle of influence gave me.

But here's also what I found:

Our Setbacks Are Setups For Success.

Today, my life is as about as abundant and glorious as life can be.

I'm happily married, with the woman of my dreams, *Robyn*. I get to spend time an incredible amount of time with my beautiful daughter, *Phoenix*. It's important that we play, and have fun, and travel, and have adventures and today, our whole family are published authors.

Little Miss Phoenix Rose Crane, is a 9-year-old 9-time bestselling author. She's also starred in a movie she wrote called *Kitty Wars*. She's also co-founded Super Kids Books Publishing, and is on a mission to help 1000 kids become super kids book authors.

Today, instead of struggling to get by, we give money and volunteer our time, to the charities we most love most.

I don't share this to brag. I'm just proud of the life we have, and quite honestly, I cherish it, because it wasn't always this way.

But no one who succeeds anything great, does it alone. You also need the right mentoring, mindset, and the right MAP, to succeed.

But really, I think it's as easy as changing the music you're listening to.

Ever get a song stuck in your head? Maybe you hum it all day. Maybe you hear it when you go to sleep at night. Maybe you made the colossal mistake of going to Disneyland and getting on the ride whose tune follows you around for days, "*It's Small World after all...*"

When you change the music and plug-in to something new you get different output.

If you aren't getting the results you want, maybe you just need to listen to a new tune.

Let this book be the right tune for you.

How to Use This Book

I structured this book like I structure my programs.

This book is built on three central beliefs:

- **You need to write a book**, and the best time to write it is—*now*. Your life *story*, your *knowledge*, and your *message* has greater importance and more market value than you probably ever imagined.

- You were put on this planet to **make a difference in the world**. The best way you can do that is to share your message with others, inside a framework that helps others succeed. (Yes, you can do this with any *topic*, or any industry.)

- There is such a thing as a "right" book. It's extremely important to your mission, your vision and your cause that you **don't waste time writing the "wrong" book**.

- Inside of these chapters, I intend to help you **discover the "right" book for you to write**. (Or, at least the right "next" book for you... but we'll talk more about that later.)

- **You can write a great book FAST**.

My suggestion, is that you tackle each chapter in order, one at a time. Each chapter comes with exercises for you to complete. What you will find is a simple, proven, step-by-step process that you can implement quickly.

Grab a pen. Take notes. And don't skip a step.

My goal is not just the you become an author, but that you build a business that gives you the freedom you desire.

Let's do this.

—Trevor

Trevor Crane
Ten Time Bestselling Author
Founder, EpicAuthor.com & SuperKidsBooks.com

If you think even a small part of you wants more help, visit this site for FREE training and support:

EpicAuthor.com/free

PREPARE

"Either write something worth reading or do something worth writing."
—**Benjamin Franklin**

ONE
Get Clarity

---

*"People don't buy WHAT you do,
they buy WHY you do it."*
—Simon Sinek

hy Write Your Book Now?

Most people struggle to start their book, and never get started.

Even fewer people finish.

Why then, is it important for *you* to write your book *now*?

Meet Viktor Frankl

An Austrian psychiatrist and Holocaust survivor, Frankl survived the Auschwitz concentration camp during World War II.

His book, *Man's Search for Meaning* has become one of the most influential books of the twentieth century. It details the author's experiences and observations while imprisoned in several different concentration camps, and pays particular attention to how finding *meaning* in even the direst of circumstances allowed him and others to survive.

Frankl's memoir has riveted generations of readers with its descriptions of life in Nazi death camps and its lessons for spiritual survival. Between 1942 and 1945, Frankl labored in four different camps, including Auschwitz, while his parents, brother, and pregnant wife perished.

Based on his own experience, Frankl argues that: **we cannot avoid suffering, but we can choose how to cope with it, find meaning in it, and move forward with renewed purpose.**

"Those who have a 'why' to live can bear with almost any 'how.'"
– Viktor Frankl, *Man's Search for Meaning*

Frankl's theory—known as logotherapy, from the Greek word logos ("meaning")—holds that our primary drive in life is not pleasure, as Freud maintained, *but the:*

Discovery and pursuit of what we personally find meaningful.

WRITE THE RIGHT BOOK FAST

"There must be a spark of the search for meaning in people. Recognize it, and presuppose it in people, and you will elicit it from people, and make him become what he in principle is capable of becoming."
—**Viktor Frankl**.

At the time of Frankl's death in 1997, *Man's Search for Meaning* had sold more than 10 million copies in 24 languages. In a reader survey, conducted by the Library of Congress, it was ranked one of the top 10 most influential books in America.

For Frankl, *meaning* came from three possible sources: purposeful <u>work</u>, <u>love</u>, and <u>courage in the face of difficulty</u>.

For him, it was the thought of seeing his wife again, returning to his work, and reconstructing his lost manuscript.

<u>What does this have to do with writing your book?</u>

Everything.

Setting yourself up to win begins with adopting the right *mindset*. Writing the "right" book begins with having that great mindset and getting clarity about the *purpose* of your book.

As Tony Robbins says, "Eighty percent of success is psychology, while twenty percent of success is mechanics."

This means that what goes on in your heart and in your mind, is more important than the mechanics, or "how-to's" of your book or your business.

Why?

Because, even if you know "how" to do something, you won't produce gratifying results if you have *inner conflicts.*

Your mind will reference ideas and experiences that are in *conflict* with your goals and dreams.

This conflict nullifies your best efforts.

Suppose you've had past experiences, in which you missed the mark and didn't achieve what you wanted. If these thoughts continue to influence your thinking—no amount of work or expertise will make you a success.

Likewise, negative and limiting ideas about "success," or "money," or "your ability to become an author," that you may have learned in the past can continue to hold sway in your thoughts and dominate your results.

You can easily short-circuit your success before you begin.

This means that your *attitude* is really more important than knowing *how* to achieve success and accomplish your goals.

Here's the good news: <u>You are in control.</u>

You can create new reference experiences that can empower your thoughts, and set yourself up to succeed. You can meet successful people and see that many of them are helpful and generous. You can read the biographies of successful people and discover that they failed many times before they achieved a great success.

One of the reasons stories are so powerful, including the stories and examples in this book, is that they help build the beliefs that you need to succeed.

In essence, you can build a whole new internal library of success resources.

The more you let your mind reference these ideas and experiences, the more you will head straight for your goal with increasing confidence.

This can help you rewire your thoughts, and do most of the "heavy lifting" for you. So long as you don't talk yourself out of the success you seek, your mind will start to make success connections for you.

This can unleash the *full power* of your inner resources. As you face new challenges, you will begin to radiate confidence and resolve. Circumstances that once fazed you will no longer faze you. You will succeed, whereas in the past you might have faltered.

Plus, the byproduct of this happy state of affairs will also begin to show up in your bank account. When you have the *right mindset* and the right *reasons*, it'll be pretty hard <u>not</u> to succeed!

ONE - GET CLARITY

Here's the question:

"Why" is it important that you write a book?

Take a moment to capture your why now. You must have strong reasons behind *why* writing your book is so important. Your why becomes the *fuel* you need to *overcome* your challenges.

It's what will get you out of bed even though it's cold outside and you just want to sleep.

_____

_____

_____

_____

Years back, after I had filed my 2.2-million-dollar bankruptcy and was living in the basement of a friend's house with my 3-year-old daughter, Phoenix, I was at my lowest point.

I was broke. I was embarrassed. I felt like a total loser.

I could have given up.

But I didn't.

I wouldn't give up on my little girl.

On my family. On my creator.

My purpose in life is to be love and to playfully, and effortlessly empower every soul I touch. To represent the idea that anyone can make anything they want of this life.

<u>I still wanted that, even when I was at my lowest.</u>

In the end, it isn't the things we have done that we remember, but the lives we've touched and the memories we have created along the way.

So, I started over from scratch with a burning desire to succeed.

Today, I am a 10-time bestselling author.

I'm madly in love with my wife. My little girl is 9 years old with 9 bestselling books. and she is building a healthy 6-figure business behind her books. (Yeah, she's only 9.)

My team and I have helped our clients generate *millions* in bottom-line profits.

The reason I'm sharing this with you is that I believe one of the *biggest reasons* I'm experiencing this level of freedom today, is because I shifted my mindset and became an author.

There are people out there who want and need your expertise.

Not to be dramatic, but in some cases, they are literally dying without it.

Let's say you found a new solution to a health-related problem, which was causing great suffering. Just like Jamie did for autistic children.

If you don't get your book done, and out there to help these people, how would it affect them?

Wouldn't you be doing them a *disservice*?

When you write a book, not only do you gain instant credibility with these people, but you begin a relationship of *trust* and *connection* with your audience.

The "right" book, won't just share your *successes*; it will share your *challenges* and vulnerability. This makes it easier for you to connect with and share that *very special gift you have*—with them.

I believe we are put on this earth to make a difference.

I don't know what your reason is, or what your *why is,* for writing your book.

Everyone has a different one.

But I do know this—*you should write it down.*

Don't wait.

Meet Pat

Pat is the #1 bestselling co-author of the book *The Miracle Morning for Network Marketers.*

Pat is also making some nice "book royalties" every month, since his book launched in September of 2015.

In January 2017, Pat's book royalties were $18,000 and growing every month.

Pat struggled while trying to write his book for nearly six months until he got "clarity" about the project and his system to create it.

When he finally figured it out, Pat got his book done—fast.

Once Pat found this "clarity," he created the outline for his book in two hours and wrote the main manuscript by speaking into his phone while taking a long four-hour walk around his neighborhood.

In six hours, he captured the first draft of his book, compared to the previous six months of wasted time and energy where he seemingly made no progress.

"After I got that outline done, I went on a walk for literally

> *about four hours, four and a half hours, with my iPhone in hand. The default voice recorder app that it's got on there just pulled up, and I was walking around the neighborhood with my outline in front of me speaking into my iPhone and recording it. I recorded each of the different chapters.* ***If you make a mistake, you just keep piling through when you're dictating like that. We took those dictations. I sent those to a service.*** *I think I used speechpad.com; I'm pretty sure."*

Within 2-3 months, Pat's book was complete.

> *"Eventually, I finally landed on a process that worked really really well for me that I'd be happy to go into if you want me to. Once we landed on that process, then I think we had the book pretty much from the beginning to end in maybe three to four months… once we got the right process the work for us …"*

I love hearing stories like this.

You can write a great book. You can create something that you care about, believe in, and get rave reviews, WITHOUT wasting time and WITHOUT having previously ever written a book. You can do it quickly.

What's needed, just like Pat said, is a PROCESS to get it done. A SYSTEM that is proven to work. One that helps you gain CLARITY on what to do first, what to do next, and so on until you have your book *done.*

In Pat's case, he learned that you must get clear enough to have an outline for your book, so you know WHAT you need to share with your reader.

He then SPOKE IT (his content) into his phone, while walking around his neighborhood.

Once he spoke it, he had it SCRIBED, and captured his FIRST DRAFT of his book within <u>six hours</u>.

When you have clarity, you can get your book done quickly.

In chapter 4, we will jump into helping you get clear about WHO you are writing the book for, WHY that audience might care about your book, and WHAT you would like to offer beyond the book. Step by step.

Authors change lives.

ACTION STEP

I'm putting the question here again:

"Why" is it important that you write a book?

Take a moment to capture your why now. You must have strong reasons behind *why* writing your book is so important. Your why becomes the *fuel* you need to *overcome* your challenges.

It's what can get you out of bed even though it's cold outside and you just want to sleep.

_____

_____

_____

_____

_____

TWO
Set Yourself Up To Win

"A man who has a why to live for can bear with almost any how."
—Friedrich Nietzsche

Meet John

Maybe you've heard of John Gray before?

He's the bestselling author of *Men Are From Mars, Women Are From Venus.*

I don't know if you're familiar with this story or not, but when John's father passed away, it happened in a pretty horrific way.

John's father was the victim of a car hijacking. The hijackers then locked his dad in the trunk of his own car. After their joyride, they left John's father in the trunk and parked the car on the side of the road.

John's dad died of asphyxiation, locked in the trunk of his own car.

When John and his brother went to pick up the car at the police impound after the incident, John had a morbid curiosity, to want to know what his father went through in his final moments.

So, John asked his brother to lock him in the trunk, just as his dad had been.

"Are you out of your mind?!?" his brother asked. But John wanted to know what his father had gone through and crawled into the trunk anyway.

There, in the trunk of the car, as John's eyes grew accustomed to the dark, he started to see what his father must have seen, and he could also see what his father tried to do to escape.

He saw how his father must have found a screwdriver to poke holes through the roof of the trunk to create air holes to breathe.

Cramped as John was, he managed to turn himself around and saw how his father had tried, unsuccessfully, to *tear* through the back seat, in a desperate attempt to claw through the cushion and into the main cab of the car.

But John could see that to escape that way wasn't possible.

Feeling helpless, John looked at the hole where his father had punched out a taillight. And as John stuck his arm out where the taillight used to be, he imagined the horror his father must have gone through, being so close to freedom, and yet so far away.

Standing outside the trunk of the car, John's brother, saw John reach his arm out and said: *"Hey John, now that I see your arm, see if you can reach over and let yourself out."*

Trapped in the trunk of the car, it hadn't even crossed John's mind.

But John reached over, and with the press of a button, opened the trunk of the car.

What was John's brother's advantage?

Was he just smarter than John?

Or, did he have a different perspective of the same problem?

You see, I believe that the "solutions" to the "problems" we have, are all around us.

Success is often not that difficult, nor do I think our problems are as complex as we make them out to be.

The real challenge is most people, most business owners, try to solve their problems by themselves. I believe, that just like John's father, we're all locked inside the trunk of our own realities.

And freedom is simply a button push away.

What can make *all* the difference is having the right *third-party perspective,* to help us discover the right solution. If we just knew the right buttons to push, we could direct our efforts and our energies with laser-focused precision.

This is why it's so important to have a team. A team has a different perspective and is there to help you win.

Success then is virtually inevitable.

Here's what I want you to do next:

Recruit a team of people who will help you win.

To get started, all you need are a few people.

I suggest you select:

- 2 Personal Partners

- 2 Professional Partners

- 2 Promotional Partners

In just a moment, I'm going to ask that you write down their names.

Don't worry about what to say to them just yet. We'll cover that next. Also, don't fret about how to get them to agree to join your team, or what you need from them.

For now, just let me explain a little more, so you're clear. Then, you can write down their names.

2 Personal

The first people to recruit for your team, are people who can help you personally.

These are people like your best friend, or spouse, or someone you love. Maybe it's your mom, your dad, or siblings.

These two people are people you can talk to, and commit to, and will help hold you *accountable* to make sure you get the book done.

Again, for now don't worry about what you're going to say to them, just write down two names:

1. _____
2. _____

Got it?

Great job. Next step.

2 Professional

If you don't have two personal names written down, go back and do it.

If you have. Let's write down another two names.

This time, write down the names of two professionals. People you can confide in, and whose opinion you value. This could be a peer. Or it could be someone you've worked with in the past. Maybe it's someone you trust or look up to.

These two will be more like your mentors, so you have someone to go to, to ask for advice. These are also people who want to see you win, and you might feel embarrassed in front of if you fail to follow through and write your book.

Seriously, write their names down before moving to the next step.

Now, if you are thinking, *but Trevor, I don't have anyone*! No problem.

If you don't know the answer of someone who's a professional, and you're struggling to think of anyone, then two things:

First - I think you need to try harder; everybody knows somebody.

Second - I invite you to apply for our Epic Author Academy program.

If you do join us, you'll get lifetime access to our own in-house publishing team, easy-to-use templates, training videos and much more. Not only will you learn how to write the right book to grow your business; you will also learn how to market it, and monetize it.

Remember, this is about growing the right team of people around you who can support you to go to the next level you want to achieve.

Write down two names now:

1. _____
2. _____

Next.

2 Promotional

I want you to write down two more names.

Two names of people who can help you *promote your book*.

I'll give you an example; it might be a good friend of yours who can broadcast, and send an email to their list, and to their networks. It could be a podcast, or radio show, or someone you know who is successful and has access to a big group of people.

Get creative; You can go to a leader in your church or community. Elicit help for your book now, while in its infancy, and people will feel as if they are part of your team, and can help collaborate with you in powerful ways to help you win.

For example, Steve Napolitan is the author of the #1 bestselling book *Capture Clients Close Deals*. He's also in our Epic Author Mentoring program, so a small group of us get together to mentor each other, and help one another with our books and in our business.

In this program, I'm also able to work personally with our members, and Steve and I worked together to get his messaging right, and his book done. Also, Steve asked me, if I would be one of his promotional partners, and I agreed.

When the time came, I sent my entire list a message telling people to get the book, and I promoted his book on all of my networks and social media channels.

*Please don't skip this step!

Write down two names for at least two promotional partners.

I really want you to experience the power, support, and confidence that comes from knowing you have a <u>team</u> behind you.

You don't need to say anything to them yet.

Just write down their names.

ACTION STEP

If you've not done so already, write down the names of the first people you're going to recruit for your new team.

2 Personal Partners

1. _____
2. _____

2 Professional Partners

1. _____
2. _____

2 Promotional Partners

1. _____
2. _____

THREE
Tell The World

"Fear is temporary regret is forever."
—Unknown

In this chapter, I'm calling you out.

I think it's time for you to tell everyone that you're writing a book.

Are you up to the challenge?

It's not hard.

Now that you have some clarity about why it's important that you get your book done; plus, you have a small team you just recruited that has, "set you up to win…"

It's time.

Tell the world you're writing a book.

Why?

Meet Lisa

Lisa Chastain is one of my wife's FEMM Mentorship clients, who decided she wanted to write a book. During our first meeting, I asked Lisa questions to help her get clear about why she wanted a book, who she wanted to write it for, etc.

Lisa was just in the initial stages of planning her book, and not really clear yet about all the details, but she knew with certainty that a book would be a powerful asset for her.

As I probed for more information about the best path for Lisa to use to write her book and grow her business, I told her what I tell all my clients: to tell the world about it.

Lisa didn't have a title, or a cover, or a well thought out *description* of her book, but she did have two things: 1. Lisa is coachable and 2. Lisa takes action.

Taking my advice, Lisa left our meeting and immediately posted on Facebook about how she'd just gotten out of a meeting with her publisher, and that she was going to finally write her book.

And Lisa took my advice again and followed up with all of the comments and support that she received on Facebook, and less than 30 days later, Lisa has closed over $12,000 worth of new business, based on only 2 Facebook posts about her book.

Are you ready to tell people about your book yet?

Now, one thing Lisa has, that you may not have yet, is she has:

1. Something to sell, and

2. A proven system to sell it.

What can I say? She's well trained.

Both of those things are covered extensively in my wife's FEMM Mentoring program, so actually, Lisa was set-up ahead of time to succeed. Lisa has also been to our Advanced Sales Mastery Event.

But that's okay. That's what we're here for. Prior to working with my wife, Lisa didn't have any of that. She went from making NOTHING to making over $25,000 in just 4 months.

Are you curious about what Lisa does?

If so, Lisa works with strong professional women who make good money but are frustrated, because they have nothing to show for it. She is creating a SISTERHOOD of like-minded women who are having incredible financial success and making an even greater impact on the world. (If you'd like to learn more about Lisa, go to: lisachastain.com)

Now, while Lisa is certainly *awesome*, her experience is not unique.

Meet Bronkar

Last year Bronkar Lee, and is wife Cyndi, hired me to help him with his (their) book.

For years, Bronkar has been an entertainer who spent much of his time on the road performing. Recently most of his gigs took place on cruise ships, which while a ton of fun, did not lend itself to a lifestyle that he wanted, with what came next.

Recently Bronkar and Cyndi got together and made a little baby-bronkar. (His name is Elijah, but I just think it's funny to call him, baby-bronkar.)

With his new son, Bronkar was seeking to shift his business so he could book more corporate speaking and training gigs, as well as grow his coaching and consulting practice.

He desired more speaking gigs, higher fees, and new coaching and consulting clients.

As Bronkar started thinking about his book and talking about his book, an interesting thing happened. He met people who booked him to speak and bought his book. (To see his book: BamTheBook.com)

Specifically, he heard this, "I love the sound of your book! I want you to be the keynote speaker at our next event, and I'll buy 225 copies."

There was only one problem. Bronkar hadn't written one word of his book. And now he had a speaking gig in 60 days, and he needed 250 books there.

(Does that sound scary to you? Or awesome?)

For Bronkar, it was a little of both.

Here's what happened:

"All I can say is BAM!!! 6 weeks ago, my book was an idea. Today, it's a #1 International Bestseller! BEFORE it was even written, it helped me book a talk show, and presell 250 copies. I've got new speaking gigs around the globe, and I've launched my first online program that's being fed by my book. I'm freaking thrilled!"
—Bronkar Lee, #1 Bestselling Author and Motivational Speaker

Broker showed up to the event with 300 copies of his new best-selling book, just to be safe.

Overall, what's Bronkar's book worth to him in dollars?

There's no telling.

Because your book is only the beginning.

The point is, even before writing his book, the act of telling people about it—or as I like to say *broadcasting it*; let's call this the "declaration" phase of your book marketing... whatever you want to call it—Bronkar grew his business.

Are you starting to see the possibilities?

Now, you actually have to do something, in order to get wins like this to show up in your life, but I hope this is feeling a little more achievable for you as well.

Just by taking the simple action of telling people you are writing a book.

Here's how you can say it,

"I'm writing a book about... (fill in the blank)".

It's not rocket science.

Below is an example. All you need to do is insert your subject.

<u>Other ways you can frame your answer:</u>

- I'm writing a book about how people can (insert the promise).

- I'm writing a book that will help people (insert the promise).

- I'm writing a book about how I overcame (insert the problem).

You don't have to be perfect. But you do need to get started.

It probably sounds better when you say it like this,

> "You don't have to be great to start,
> but you have to start to be great."
> —Zig Ziglar

Here's one more example.

<u>Meet Robyn</u>

FYI - Robyn is my wife.

When Robyn first told the world she was writing a book; it was about a subject she came up with called, *Money Parenting*.

Just an aside, this was the subject that helped Robyn breakthrough and earn her first six-figures in her business. Thinking that the parents of young children would be interested in her subject, Robyn would speak any place she could: kindergartens, preschools, churches, and synagogues, etc.

But here's what happened for Robyn.

She started interviewing people for her new book, and her referrals kept leading to better and better connections, and introductions, and before long, Robyn decided to change her brand and her message. She decided to write a different book. The *Money Parenting Book* she thought to write originally, was no longer the "right" book for her target audience.

Around the same time, Robyn began telling people about her new book, she was asked to be on an online TV show, she started her own radio show, and she began a new podcast. Her brand began to grow. Was it all because she was celebrating the book? No, but it definitely helped.

Robyn had a talk at a Tony Robbins New York Power Team meeting in NYC. Her book was complete, but the paperback had yet to arrive.

Guess what happened?

From that one "free" talk, in front of about 50 people, Robyn closed over $35,000 worth of new business. How did she leverage the book? Because she didn't have the books in hand yet, she printed a paper dust-cover version of the cover of her book, wrapped it around a different book, and held it up in the front of the room.

Oh, and she offered a free copy to anyone who chose to work with her.

I hope you're ready to take this step seriously.

If you are, then go tell the world.

Post on Facebook, LinkedIn, Twitter, and Instagram. Make some videos. Call people. Include that you're the "Forthcoming Author of, *Your Awesome Book Title*" at the bottom of your emails.

My first declaration was to my mom! "Hey Mom, I'm writing a book!"

If this step freaks you out, that's okay.

It's a little freaky.

Because when you put it out there, it makes it real. I hope you're uncomfortable. If you're not, then I suggest you take it up a notch and do something that does stretch you.

Make your desire to succeed greater than your fear of change.

What if you're still confused about your book?

That's okay.

You can still do this.

You can just say, "I'm writing a book. I haven't decided what the subject is yet. But I'm really going to get this done."

The whole point is to *declare* you're writing a book!

One more thing:

In the last chapter, you were asked to write down some specific names of people you can contact and add to your team.

Here's what you can say to recruit people on your team.

> For your personal contacts:
>
> Buy them pizza and beer. Just kidding. I don't need to tell you what to do with your family and friends…just ask for their help. Maybe something like this…

"Hi Mom, this is (insert your name). Can I ask you a favor? I've decided to write a book, and my publisher told me I have to get two people who are friends or family members who could support me and help hold me accountable. Would you be my number one? *(Never call your mom number two.)*

For your professional contacts:

Again, this is up to you. But if you look up to someone, one of the best ways to get their attention, is to one-compliment them, and two-ask for advice.

Successful people are almost always ready to help if you ask properly. So, set your sights high, and go talk to some people. You might say,

"Hi Joe, this is (insert your name). Do you have a few minutes to talk? The reason I'm calling you is that out of all the people I ever worked with at XYZ company, you were not only the coolest, but you seemed to be the most intelligent person on the staff. I was just curious if I could get your advice about something?"

After they agree, then just tell them you've decided to write a book, and you were curious if they'd be willing to advise and/or support you during the process. Be open-hearted and honest about why you're writing a book, and why you'd value their assistance.

For your promotional contacts:

Same advice here, as you would use with your professional contacts. Feed them a compliment/favor or even a sandwich, and watch people line up to help you. You might say,

"Hi Sue, this is (insert your name). I've been a big fan of your podcast for quite a while now, and I was wondering if I could ask you a favor? You see, my publisher asked me to identify who I thought were the most successful, and influential people I could find, who have the coolest following, and then to ask them if they'd be willing to mention my new book to their audience if I agreed to give it away for free. And for every book I send out, I'll make a donation to XYZ charity. (Hint—pick their favorite charity.)

ACTION STEP

1. In the next 24 hours, announce on social media that you're writing a book.

2. Reach out to at least two, if not all six of the people you added to your list from the last chapter.

3. Ready… set… go!

PLAN

*"Your gifts are limitless.
Don't be afraid to let them shine."*
—Trevor Crane

FOUR
Strategy

"All things being equal, the simplest explanation is most likely the correct one."
—Occam's Razor

When I was 20 years old, my friends and family said I should write a book.

Having spent my entire life in my small hometown of Cave Creek, Arizona, I had just returned from an almost two-year trip backpacking around the world. I'd kept a journal, plus my family had kept the letters I'd sent home, so inspired by friends we came up with a possible title, *A Backpack and a Smile*.

I never got that book done.

When I was 30 years of age, I wanted to write a book. By then, I had a successful water sports business. I had this great idea about how I was going to help people. My draft title for that book was, *A Dollar's Not a Tip, and the Beach Is Not Your Ash Tray*.

I never wrote that book.

At 33, I wanted to write a book to help advance my business.

FOUR - STRATEGY

But then I thought, "Who would ever want a book written by me when I hadn't created anything *substantial* yet?"

So, I never wrote that book.

Eventually, my business success was super-charged. I didn't have a book, but I had all this success: cars, houses, traveling the world, etc. Then, again, I had clients, and I had friends and family saying, "Hey, you should write a book!"

But then I had *no time* to write a book.

It was one excuse after another.

I didn't consider myself a writer, so I didn't know "*how*" to write, or what my content *could* or *should* be.

I wasn't sure who should read the book, and I sure as hell didn't know how it would help my career or business, or how I would make money from it.

I was frustrated and confused.

Sure, I'd had these willy-nilly ideas about writing a book.

But that's it.

They just *stayed* ideas.

But it didn't need to be that way.

If I only knew then, what I know today, I would have written several of those books years ago.

Regretfully, we can't go back in time.

Our only choice is to make the most of the time we have left.

Let me show you where to <u>start,</u> so you don't waste years (like I did) thinking about writing a book, but not actually getting it done (or even started).

This may seem counterintuitive, but the secret to writing the RIGHT book fast (and to growing your business, as well) is to start—*at the end.*

One of the reasons people don't get started, and CERTAINLY a reason people don't finish, is they don't have clarity about WHERE they are going, HOW they are going to get there, and WHY it's so important to push through all the bullshit that will inevitably pop up and stand in your path, and seemingly conspire to never let you succeed.

It begins with clarity.

This is not just about the clarity of your purpose or your "WHY" behind writing the book (as discussed in Chapter 1), but If you want to get from location A to B, and you've never been to location B before, you need a map. Or, GPS…or Google.

This means you need total clarity about "where you are" and "where you want to be."

You need to know the "*path,*" specifically the steps along the way, the instructions on how to get from "here" to "there." Depending on where you want to go, there are many different vehicles you could use to get there. Perhaps, you'd travel by car, or ferry, or bus, or plane, or by foot.

Same thing with your book.

And let me assure you, there are <u>steps</u> to take to get you from "*blank page*" to "*your awesome book*"—in 90 days or less.

The diagram on the next page illustrates this.

<u>The steps in order are:</u>

- Strategy.
- Structure.
- Story.
- Set a Date.
- Speak.
- Scribe.
- Source.

<u>In this chapter, I will explain the seven steps illustrated in the diagram.</u>

This will help you see the big picture, and start familiarizing yourself with our Epic Author System.

We will also dive deeper into each element, to help you take *specific* and *simple steps* to arrive at your end result… Yes, you'll have a great book. But ultimately, I want you to have all the rewards that come along with it.

If you don't write the RIGHT book, and you don't know how to *<u>effectively</u>* use it, and *<u>leverage</u>* it, to get what you want, it becomes a *useless* and therefore, a *worthless* tool.

Instead, let me show you how to **write a book that you'll be proud of,** and one that will help you get the RESULTS you want from having that book—*faster than you would have imagined.*

Had I known these earlier, I wouldn't have held myself back from getting my book(s) done a long time ago.

Now, it's your turn.

Figure 1 - Epic Author System

STEP #1: Strategy

The first step is to get clarity.

Here's why:

Before my grandfather died at 92, he wrote me a letter. It was the last letter he ever wrote me. In that letter, he sent me a synopsis of his nearly-a-century's worth of advice on living a *great* life.

My grandpa shared his best memories and listed the most magical moments he felt had made his life magnificent.

He died with few regrets.

But his letter stirred something inside of me.

After he passed away, I re-read his letter and cried tears of gratitude. Inside his letter, was a pattern I recognized that inspired me to make changes in my life that I could use to commit to becoming my best, and the required components to make the best of your life.

My grandfather's words changed my life.

Eventually, I started an online-TV show and podcast inspired by his letter, which also inspired a book I wrote, called *Greatness Quest*.

Now, as much as this concept fired me up, and as much as I LOVED the idea of this book and had the desire to share this story… it wasn't the first book I chose to write.

Why?

Because it was missing something.

FOUR - STRATEGY

I didn't have a clear understanding about some core questions, and just as importantly I didn't have *answers to wh*at I'm going to share with you in this chapter.

By the way, I didn't figure this out on my own. I got help. I had a mentor, or mentors, really, who supported me and challenged me and helped me ask and answer the hard questions.

Even today, I can't imagine trying to do this without guidance—and now I have 10 books.

Here's what I didn't know…

4 Key Questions:

To make sure you write the right book, you need to get clarity about the answers to these 4 Key Questions.

1. Who is the book for?
2. What is it about?
3. Why do they care? *(2 parts: problems and results)*
4. What do you want them to do next?

WARNING: These may seem like simple questions, but you'd be surprised how difficult it can be to properly answer these questions, and then figure out how to articulate your answers to other people.

I'll go into these in more detail in a minute, but first, because I didn't know, and couldn't figure out the answers to these questions, I chose <u>not</u> to make my first book be about the lessons I learned from my grandfather.

Now, let me add one more thing.

I've stated all over this book, how important it is to write what I refer to as the RIGHT book.

At this point, you might be wondering, "What is the RIGHT book?"

Allow me to explain that now.

First of all, having the "right" book means that when everything is said and done, that you are PROUD of your book. All too often, nearly every day, I meet people who are <u>not</u> proud of their books.

They don't think they're good enough, or they don't know how to use them within their business, or to get speaking gigs, or whatever their expectations were…they are not met.

Often, they self-sabotage the value of their books, because they start describing ways it could have been better, or that it wasn't published by a traditional publisher, or it's only an ebook, etc.

Often, they feel like they've wasted their time, their effort, and their energy.

That is <u>not</u> the right book.

As I said, the "right" book is one that you are PROUD of. It's one that you can use to position your expertise and authority around a particular subject matter. It's a book that can become your most powerful marketing tool. It leads people you want to work with, to want to work with you. It generates quality leads for your business, and it opens doors to new clients, new partnerships, new marketing, and media opportunities.

Having the right book is life changing.

To make sure you're writing the "right" book, make sure it has "The Right Stuff."

<u>The three criteria to make sure your book has "The Right Stuff":</u>

1. It positions you as an expert
2. It generates leads
3. It helps you grow your business, or further your cause

If your book doesn't do those things, then I don't think it's the right book for you to write, *at least not the FIRST book you want to write.*

Notice, that I told you the story about my grandfather? And my burning desire to write a book about the lessons he shared with me? Well, eventually I *did* write that book.

It just wasn't the *first* book I wrote.

Why? Because I didn't know the answers to the "4 Key Questions," and my book idea didn't have "The Right Stuff." Only when I had answered those questions and met the criteria for having "The Right Stuff," did I actually write the book.

Please allow me to also take a little bit of the pressure off you.

You're not going to write just *one* book.

Instead, especially once you understand this process, you'll most likely have *many* books.

The question is, what's the *first* book you're going to write?

This is great news!

Now, you don't have to focus on making sure you STUFF everything you've ever learned and include every story that's ever shaped you into your awesome self, into just one book.

This means you can keep coming up with great ideas, and things you're passionate about, and **keep being passionate about them!**

Capture those great ideas. Write them down. Add them to your journal or calendar, and one day, you can write those books.

When you're ready.

How do you know you're writing the RIGHT book?

1. You ask and answer the "4 Key Questions," and
2. Meet the three criteria to making sure your book has "The Right Stuff."

This is to help ensure you know how to "use" your book, and "leverage" your book, and that you can feel "proud" of your book.

Instead of writing a book about my grandfather, I looked at what I was best at. I considered the biggest, and baddest results that I've created for other people. I considered who I most wanted to work with. And I discovered my answer.

It came down to what I was already doing.

I was *already* coaching and consulting with business owners to help them generate more revenue or make more sales. The biggest result I helped my clients create was to help them systematically close high-ticket sales.

Personally, I've found it takes just as much effort to sell something for a dollar, as it takes to sell something for hundreds or thousands of dollars. The only difference was, I got paid more.

That is what people were paying me for. That's what I was best at.

But, I'll tell you, I was a little bit scared to put all my trade secrets and high-level strategies into the book. I thought, *why would anyone hire me if I put it all in my book?*

So, if you ever start to feel that way, know I've been there. **And trust me, don't worry about that crap.** You don't have to be concerned about putting too much mojo into your book. You virtually *can't* give away the keys to the kingdom.

See, what most people don't realize is (and I've said it before, and I'll say it again here) is that...

Your book is only the beginning.

If your book is the "end," then in all honestly, you are HURTING people, by not giving them the next-level support they need to implement your awesomeness into their lives.

Here's what I did.

I went through the same process you are going through in this book, except you'll be able to do it faster than I did because we have improved and simplified the system.

So, I decided that the *first book* I would write would be called *High-Paying Clients*.

"Getting high-paying clients" was the RESULT people hired me for.

This is important.

Because, as I've shared, the first book you *want* to write, might not be the first book you *need* to write.

Sure, *Greatness Quest* was about personal empowerment, which I'm phenomenal at, by the way. But what I was *best* at providing (at the time), and the thing that people were *happily* paying me for... was helping them get high-paying clients.

Now, I'm not saying you shouldn't feel *inspired* by your book. In fact, I think it's important that you're passionate about your subject, and that you use that as rocket fuel to ignite your success.

I'm just saying that you should keep "the end in mind" when you begin. Then you follow a system that works. Be systematic about it. Be strategic. Be smart.

If you were completing a jigsaw puzzle, isn't it helpful to know what the final image looks like?

Don't make the **mistake** that almost *everyone* does when they start writing a book. They start writing their life's *story*. They talk about all the things that happened in their life.

In the context of writing the "right" book, it's like trying to stuff a square peg, into a round hole.

If you do that, you're wasting your time.

Because not all of your stories are relevant.

I believe you should write a *book* to *grow your business, or forward your cause.*

When it comes time, you will add all the relevant stories that you need in your book to prove the points you want to make.

Typically, I don't suggest you "start" with your stories. Instead, you add them into your book, as if they are precious diamonds, and you are the jeweler who carefully and artfully selects the right diamonds, and inserts them in exactly the right places.

Always, start with the end in mind.

So, consider this next question. I ask this next question a lot, because, **soon you're going to have a new problem.**

Once your book is done, "Now what?"

Imagine holding it in your hand…it's all done.

You're proud of it. It's got a great title, and cover, and you know exactly the type of person you wish would read it.

What are you going to do next?

Order 500 copies? Or, 5,000 copies?

Then what?

Lick stamps and mail them out one at a time?

It's a quality question, but one people rarely consider or understand until they're faced with it…but, it's coming.

Your book will get done.

And if you haven't thought your strategy all the way through, you're going to find it extremely difficult to turn your book into the powerful marketing tool you'd like it to be.

So, imagine your phenomenal book is done 90 days from today. **You did it.**

Congratulations. Now…

<u>**Brainstorm the answers to these questions:**</u>

- What are you going to sell with your book?
- How will your book make you a profit?
- What will people *pay* you to help them with?

- What product will people *buy* from you?
- Who are you writing it for?
- What do they currently think?
- What do they need to know?
- What do you want your readers to get?
- What actions do you want your readers to take next?

<u>Here's a few more:</u>

- "What are you best at?"
- "Who do you love working with?"
- "What are the biggest and most awesome results that you already create for people?"
- "What problems are you great at solving?"

Thinking these things through, with the end in mind, is being *strategic*.

Strategy is the intelligent pathway to get to your end goal; fast and effectively.

This means minimizing what's not needed and focusing on what is. In the cockpit of an airplane, there are hundreds of spinning dials. Yet only 2-3 are *necessary* for the pilot to focus on at any one time.

Hal Moore Jr., a retired United States Army Lieutenant General, recipient of the Distinguished Service Cross (U.S. military's second highest decoration), and author, simplifies it into two basic questions:

- What am I doing that I shouldn't be doing?
- What am I not doing that I should be doing?

Now, it might seem strange at first, considering that in this stage, you actually aren't even *writing* your book yet. Perhaps you might even feel that you aren't making *any* progress.

But when you take the time to plan strategically, you save yourself a significant amount of *time and energy and money and frustration*.

I suggest you only do what you <u>need</u> to do, and you <u>stop</u> doing what you <u>shouldn't</u> be doing.

I'll give you an example.

<u>Meet Jess</u>

Jess Todtfeld is a client of ours. (I always seem to be dragging on about his successes—because it's so cool!) He became a #1 bestselling author within 24 hours of launching his book *Media Secrets: A Media Training Crash Course.*

During that same time, he up-sold over a DOZEN people into the pre-launch of his brand new $1,000 program. Plus he got multiple requests to write for and to be featured in major media around the world.

What created this?

A few things.

Jess was *clear* on his purpose (his why which we covered in the first chapter), and he was clear on his strategy. He planned it out with me for two months.

He knew what customers were going to buy from him, he knew what he was going to write about, and he knew what he was going to sell off the back of his book.

And he *communicated* the right message to the right people.

As a direct result, Jess made significantly more money than he invested in our Epic Author Academy and Mentoring programs.

So, when contemplating your strategy, consider this:

Your book should make you a profit.

But in order to do that, you must make an offer to your readers. You've got to have a path for them to follow. *Remember, this is about writing a book to grow your business, and/or forward your cause.*

Your "mission" and "monetization" are not mutually exclusive.

They go hand in hand.

Without one, you can't have the other.

Meet Al

Years ago, I watched Al Gore give a great speech about global warming. Apparently, the world was melting, and Al was there to tell us about it. After I watched and listened to his speech, I was so moved, and so fired up; I wanted to jump into action.

I was like, "Oh my gosh, the world is melting! I want to help. Tell me, Al Gore, what can I do?"

But Al Gore didn't answer. He just finished his video and drove away in his Prius. Nothing else. There was no call to action at the end, and worse—***there was nothing for me to go do.***

I was confused, thinking, "Okay. You sold me. The world is melting. Global warming is a big problem. I want to make a difference. What can I do next to make it better?"

I never found out. Because at the end of Al Gore's damned presentation, he gave me zippo, nada, nothing.

I even looked online to try to find something. I searched, and I searched, and here's what I found out: "Replace my lights with fluorescent light bulbs." And, "Buy a Prius."

What?!

I was pissed off.

I was soooo disappointed.

I was like, "Screw you, Al Gore. What am I supposed to do to help?!

He got me all fired up, but gave me no place to go.

Think BIGGER than your book.
Support people in taking their next steps.

ACTION STEP

List the next steps you would like your readers to take during or after reading your book.

_____
_____
_____
_____
_____
_____

FIVE
Structure & Story

"Tell me the facts and I'll learn. Tell me the truth and I'll believe. But tell me a story and it will live in my heart forever."
—Native American Proverb

Few people write books.

Those who start, rarely finish.

Most people reading this, I daresay, won't finish this book. They won't follow through.

That's not to be mean, or cynical; it's a reality. But, this reality, is also your opportunity.

It only plays to *your* benefit!

Having a great book shows you follow through. Writing the right book gives you exclusive membership into a club that 98 percent of people will never join…authorship. Your book differentiates you, and in many situations, eliminates your competition, and makes the most of their attempts to one-up you, to make you insignificant.

Talk to any successful entrepreneur or investor, and they will tell you that their success didn't come by accident. They invested in what they've accomplished. It takes time, money, energy and an obsessive focus that borders on insanity.

Ideas are one thing. Execution is everything.

It's about <u>getting it done</u>.

The difference isn't just *knowing* "how" to reach a level of success. We're plagued with "how-to's" about diet, and weight loss, and relationships, and making money… there are countless books about *strategies* for success.

It's those who ACT, who make a difference.

The difference is ACTION!

What differentiates you is not whether or not you're having the dream, it's whether or not you're *living the dream*.

I really want you to understand this. I really believe that you are just <u>one book</u> away from amazing and transformational success in your business and your life.

Today, opportunities find me simply because of my book.

<u>Meet Gennadi and Alla</u>

Alla was watching the weather channel.

Apparently, an ad run by a client of mine, to promote "his" business, was being replayed there. A video was playing of my client talking about his recent success, and he mentioned my name. Alla heard the story, remembered my name and looked me up.

Since Google loves Amazon, as it is a highly credible source for relevant and powerful keyword and SEO data, one of the first things that popped up about me was my book.

Subsequently, she bought one of my books, read it and shared it with her husband. Three days later, I was on the phone with Gennadi and Alla, and they hired me to help them with their business.

After that initial meeting, they asked me to *partner* up with them, to negotiate a *multi-million-dollar deal* in New York City.

At the time of this writing, they've offered me 20 percent of a multi-million-dollar deal.

What's the Return On Investment (ROI) on that?

And, the opportunities keep coming in.

The great thing is, you'll get to *choose* whether or not you'll want to take on new clients. No more chasing. They come to you. You choose. *That's empowering.*

Contrast that with what I had to go through before I had my books?

At one point, I missed 20 sales in a row.

I'll admit it, after the 20th "No," I cried. I was so upset because I knew I could help the people I was meeting with; I just couldn't convince them to hire me.

With a book, a lot of that is *done for you.*

As you will discover in this book, people from all walks of life, with all types of businesses and causes, are experiencing similar, and often *better,* results.

Your PHENOMENAL success is next.

Meet Jeff

Jeffrey Slayter, bestselling author of *Raise Your Rates*, is a tremendously successful coach and international speaker. He has positively impacted and transformed millions of lives around the world. He's an American living in Australia, who works with clients all over the world and earns millions per year.

Meet Steve

After Steve Napolitan published his book, and it became a #1 bestseller, he was invited to C-Suite, an elite business community of C-level executives of centi-million and billion dollar businesses.

Steve was *positioned* as an authority on business growth, sales, and personal freedom!

He didn't pitch himself. He was invited.

Today, he's broken the $100K/month club, and he gets to hand-pick the best speaking gigs, the best partners, and the best clients.

The list of success stories could go on and on and fill several books.

This isn't a <u>luck</u> game. They didn't get lucky. They wrote a book. The right book. One that *grows their businesses.*

When you get the right book done, and follow the steps I'm sharing with you; you can win. Get some help, and your success is *virtually* guaranteed.

It's easier to make sales. It's easier to book gigs. You can raise your rates. And you can gain free publicity and media attention.

But it is up to you to execute.

Remember, you're not alone.

When you're ready, we have a team, and a system to support you.

Now, why all the stories?

You might be wondering how any of this relates to this chapter and the "structure" and "stories" of your book. Here's why I'm leading this section with so many stories.

Stories will motivate you into action.

And, none of the content I teach in this book will matter, if you're not inspired and motivated to get your book done!

There's a saying that I think holds very true, "Facts tell, and stories sell."

It's true.

In this chapter, I want to show you how to organize your content in an outline, soon to be your table of contents, so that your book can effectively connect with, and communicate with your future reader in such a way, that they fall in love with you and decide they want more.

The secret?

First, organize your content, and then fill it in with stories.

Let's structure your message.

Once you know the answers to the "4 Key Questions," you'll hopefully have a good idea about what your book should be about.

Once you've determined that one of the first things we want you to create is your cover.

Your cover needs to be the bait. Don't let anyone tell you otherwise. Your cover is IMPORTANT. It is the most read page of your book. It must appeal to the *right* person, get their *attention*, and trigger them to *care enough* to look a little deeper.

That's based on what it looks like and what words are used.

We do this by coming up with ideas for the *Title* and the *Subtitle*. After that, we come up with the description and message for the back of your book.

A great title and subtitle create interest and intrigue.

I like to pick titles that promise the *results* that people want, so they can avoid the *problems* that they don't want.

The visual *design* elements of the cover all work to *support* the broadcasting of this message.

The cover (front and back) of your book, broadcasts your promise.

It communicates the problem you are going to solve. And it communicates it in the language your audience will connect with.

After the cover is done, we look at structuring the inside of the book. We do this first by *creating a table of contents*. This outlines your content.

It is a logical progression that takes your reader from point A to Point B. The *table of contents*, in fact, tells your reader a story as well. It lays out the *road map* for them to get from where they are to where they want to go.

The table of contents grabs the attention of the people who want what you've promised. They want your solution, and outlining it for them makes them feel reassured that they'll get it.

So you need to ask yourself:

- Where is the reader at now?
- Where do they need to be by the time they finish your book?

After you have that clear, you then ask yourself:

- What does the reader need to know first?
- What action do they need to take first?
- What do they then need to know next?
- What is the next action they need to take?

Etcetera. Etcetera.

Until they get to the end!

This is the structure.

This is how you will know what goes in the introduction, what goes in Chapter 1 of your book, then Chapter 2, and so on.

Once you understand the strategy and purpose of your book, the structure becomes clear.

Let's discuss structuring your book in more detail.

Your Title and Subtitle

You need a great title for your book to be marketable. It's the phrase that people are going to say over and over when recommending your book to friends or talking about it on blogs.

If you have a great title—one that's easy to remember and enjoyable to say—you've already won half of the marketing battle.

The goal of the title is to reveal your book's main concept. Great titles are usually 1-5 words long such as: *Outliers*, *Harry Potter*, and *Chicken Soup for the Soul*. Any longer than that and it starts to lose its memorability. But even then, there are exceptions to the rule. Such as with books: *Men are from Mars Women are from Venus*, and *How to Win Friends and Influence People*.

The point is, if you can keep it short. And if it is more effective to make it longer, do that, too. Just *don't* insert any unnecessary wording.

Let's give you some examples.

Capture Clients Close Deals is Steve Napolitan's bestselling book. It's clearly about sales. Especially for those who are looking to gain more clients, and close more deals.

Also, keep in mind that the *subtitle* can help you communicate more of your promise, as well as connect with the problem(s) your target reader is experiencing.

They work together. The big title captures their attention. The subtitle then reinforces the problem and the promise.

So in *Capture Clients Close Deals*, the subtitle is *A Simple Way to Gain Clients Without Convincing or Chasing*. Perfect! It talks about gaining more clients (the result), and identifies the problem that it solves: you don't need to convince or chase!

I'll give you another example.

I love using the example of Tim Ferris's book *"The 4-Hour Work Week."* (FYI - It's a phenomenal book.) But the title says it all.

What's is the book about, and what _result_ or promise might the book deliver?

Well… based on the title, it looks like a "4-Hour Work Week."

But it getss better.

Let's look at the subtitle: *"Escape the 9-5, Live Anywhere, and Join the New Rich."*

What's the _problem_ the book addresses?

I don't want to give you the answer yet.

Please read the subtitle again: *"Escape the 9-5, Live Anywhere, and Join the New Rich."*

What words address the _problem_?

"Escape the 9-to-5"

What does that phrase presuppose?

It presupposes that a 9 to 5 work week is something that needs to be "escaped" from. Typically, what do people need to *escape* from?

Good stuff or bad stuff?

It's suggesting a 40-hour work week is like a *prison*, one that people can *escape from*.

***Who* is the book for?**

People working 9 to 5, and who want to escape.

What *results* does the book promise they can get?

Live Anywhere and Join the New Rich.

Tim's title and subtitle are all about:

Time freedom, location freedom, and financial freedom.

Beautiful.

Well done, Mr. Ferris.

Your Title:

Take a look at a some of the successful books that you like, like Steve's and Tim Ferris' books, and model their titles and subtitles.

Find all the books you love. Even better, go to *The New York Times Bestseller List*, or the *Amazon Best Seller List*. And choose the books with titles and subtitles that really *stand out* for you.

Model what's already working.

Place them on a coffee table if you can. Somewhere you can look at all the front covers, the spines, and what's on the *back* of the books.

If you don't want to buy the hardcopy, take a photograph of the books. You can even walk into a bookstore and do this.

Or take snapshots on your computer, and place them side-by-side.

If it is weight loss, you could model Steve Napolitan's book, and come up with the following:

- **Title:** Eat More. Weigh Less.
- **Subtitle:** A Fun Way to Get Slim Without Starving Yourself.

Or it could be, if you modeled Tim Ferris

- **Title:** The 6-Meal Day
- **Subtitle:** Eat More Food, Lose More Weight, Look Great… 30 Days or Less!

This works no matter what business you're in. And for any subject.

If you completed the previous chapter on understanding *who* you want to buy your book, *why* they might want to buy it, and *what* the result is they will get…then you can simply use those answers to come up with some title and subtitle options.

You aren't going to come up with just one.

You are going to come up with <u>at least 10</u>, preferably 20 different titles. **You can refine them, and improve them later.**

You don't have to be perfect at this. When you're starting out, you're just brainstorming. Nothing is right; nothing's wrong; it's all just ideas.

Here's a good checklist to test if your titles are marketable:

1. Write down at least 10 titles. 20 would be better.
2. Pick the top 3.
3. Share them with people.

4. Get their feedback.

Share them with everyone.

Share them with your new team, as we discussed Chapter 2; share them on social media; share them with your clients, and prospects…the importance of this is to 1. communicate and 2. get feedback. (This is marketing.)

A good checklist to use to know if your titles are marketable is as follows:

- Is this title easy to remember?
- Does it reveal the main concept or type of experience my book must offer?
- Does the title express what type of reader will benefit from reading the book?
- Does the title provoke the reader to purchase?
- Would readers enjoy recommending this title to friends?
- Does the title start a conversation when people hear it for the first time?
- Would it be easy to turn this title into a franchise, or sequel? (*Harry Potter and the…*, *The 4-Hour…*)
- Is the domain available? (Convenient, but not required.)
- Are there any other books or copyrighted material with this same title?

Ask people these questions when you share your ideas with them.

If you answered "No" to some of those questions, that's okay.

Keep brainstorming.

Eventually, you'll hit upon a winning title. Most likely, you'll probably find that winning title, from the feedback you get from other people.

Think of it like crowd-sourcing.

Other people will help you come up with an even better title and subtitle than you could come up with on your own.

This process also has you engaging in one of the most important things you need to consider about your new book…*marketing*.

As I've said, *marketing*, is begins by communicating with other people. When you engage people, and get their contribution in helping you create your book, it can help you grow your audience and expand your reach.

It also builds a deeper level of *connection* with your friends and your fans. People like to buy from people they *know*, *like* and *trust*. This interaction helps you build all three.

Meet Charles

Charles "Charlie" Hoehn, is an American bestselling author, who's done the same thing.

In his words:

> I thought about just calling my book "How I Cured My Anxiety," based on a popular post I wrote. Then I had a conversation about it with my friend Tucker Max (bestselling author of I Hope They Serve Beer in Hell), and he offered his thoughts …

> *The problem with calling it "How I Cured My Anxiety" is that it hinders word-of-mouth. Think about it: if someone wants to give your book to their friend, what are they going to say? 'Hey man, I have a great book that you need to read—it's called How I Cured My Anxiety?' That's uncomfortable because it almost sounds accusatory. 'What do you mean I should read it? You think I have anxiety?' That's not a conversation an anxious person wants to have.*

Charlie's mentor was right. So, he toyed with several other ideas:

- How to Recover from Burnout
- The 4-Week Plan for Health and Happiness
- Overcoming 'Workaholicism'

The winning title ended up being *Play It Away*.

Your Subtitle:

Do the same for the subtitle, as you did for the title. With subtitles, think of *keywords* that your ideal audience would use to search for your book on Google or Amazon. This is simple. For two reasons:

1. You've already gotten into the heads of your target reader in the *Strategy* section of planning in this book. Remember their problem, and the result they are looking for.

2. You can *Google* something or *look* at Amazon to see what people are searching already. In my Epic Author Academy online program, I provide *software* bonuses, that are research tools to help you figure out what these keywords are.

Include these keywords in your subtitle. You can have a longer subtitle if it helps you achieve this. Up to 20 words even!

So, do the following:

1. Write down at least 10 subtitles. 20 would be better.
2. Pick the top 3.
3. Share them with people.
4. Get their feedback.

Then try *different* combinations of subtitles with titles.

For the book *Play It Away*, the subtitle was simply a matter of tacking on who the book was for (workaholics), and how the book could benefit them (cure their anxiety). Thus, came the subtitle: *A Workaholic's Cure for Anxiety*.

The result was as follows:

- **Title:** Play it Away
- **Subtitle:** A Workaholic's Cure for Anxiety

Bonus Tip: If you have a working title and subtitle now, you can skip right to the part where you spread the word. Share it with people, and get their feedback.

Crafting Your Cover

I like to look at a lot of different covers. This helps me, which helps you **model the covers you like most.**

In my Epic Author Academy, I give all the members a photo of all the number one bestsellers for the year on Amazon and *The New York Times*. We use these pictures, so our community can model them. I even took photographs of the inside of the books, so you can model and map the look and feel of the format, table of contents, author page, bonuses, etc.

Your cover is vital.

It must be compelling, sophisticated and eye-grabbing. Enough that people want to click it and read the Amazon description.

I'm going to cover this by using Charlie Hoehn as an example. Charlie is a bestselling author and speaker.

He had a concept in mind for his book's cover.

It was about playing catch on a grassy hill, on a summer's day.

He wanted the color to fall somewhere between the movie posters for *Field of Dreams* and *Big Fish*. These two films for him, always felt magical, nostalgic, and playful.

Notice that he is *modeling* what has already worked. And he knows *exactly* what he wants to communicate to his target reader.

This is what he had in mind from the start.

The goal was to *instantly* communicate those qualities while revealing that the book was for anxious workaholics.

From there, Charlie decided to do a photo shoot so he could make a few cover mockups himself. That way, he would be able to quickly see if my ideas were working or not.

Here are some of his mock-ups:

WRITE THE RIGHT BOOK FAST

He handed the mockups over to a designer, who sent this back to him <u>only</u> two hours later:

In Charlie's words:

> *"No one understands the spirit and meaning of the book better than the person who wrote it. All authors should try to envision*

the exact cover they want (and how it will look when listed on Amazon), then sketch it out on paper or create a mock-up in Photoshop."

You are going to do this, too.

The Front Cover

1. Find some sample designs, and create a mock-up. You can do this by simply sketching it out on paper, or if you are savvy with Photoshop, do that, too.

    The clearer you are on the vision you want for your book, the clearer you can communicate it to a designer. And the clearer you are, the easier it is for the designer to do their job. This saves you both *time* and *money*!

    Remember, you don't have to do this alone! Even if your designs are *terrible* sketches on a napkin, you can hire a *great* designer on upwork.com or 99Designs.com or even fiverr.com who can turn your ideas into something beautiful.

    Make sure you get at least the mock-ups. Preferably five. After that, you are going to do the following:

2. Show the mock-ups to your friends, potential customers, and colleagues. Get them to vote on the cover they like best.

    Again, you don't have to guess! You get *feedback* from people. You broadcast this and get opinions via email, social media, or even in person.

    My preference is to do it using *Facebook*. It's easy to get people's feedback there.

    This is also one of the benefits of being a part of the Epic

Author Academy. There, we walk you through getting the right title, subtitle, and book cover for your book.

And, you can get FEEDBACK from the specialized community regarding which one works best. Not just from anyone. But from like-minded business builders who want to *grow their business* by *writing their books*.

The Back Cover

I'm going to continue using *Charlie Hoehn* as a case study for this. Notice, I am even modeling the success of others' in teaching you what to do!

Why?

Because it works.

It's about getting out of my ego, and focusing on what *you* as the reader needs.

So, the description of your book goes on your back cover. A fuller description. It's the blurb. It's what also gets people to *buy* the book. Once the cover design, title, and subtitles hook them, they are going to want to find out more about the book.

This is the next step.

Now, the back cover really is the *deal breaker* as to whether someone buys your book or not.

It's the sales pitch that converts an *interested* lead into a paid customer.

The great thing is, we already understand our target reader. Remember in the strategy section; we got clear on *who* you want to read it, *why* they ought to read it, and *what* result they would get?

We even asked you to *survey* them, so you understand exactly where they are in life, the way they think, and even the words they use.

This <u>all</u> helps you formulate your back cover. Notice that every step of the Epic Author System you have taken builds on another.

No surprise, Charlie Hoehn took those serious steps, too.

He went and surveyed about *130* people to get their thoughts on his following questions:

1. In your own words, describe what your anxiety feels like. How does it manifest itself? In what situations does it arise?

2. What solutions have you tried in the past to manage your anxiety? What's worked, and what didn't work? How did you feel before and after trying these solutions?

3. What is the biggest obstacle that's preventing you from getting your anxiety under control?

4. What would it mean to you if you got your anxiety under control? How would things change? What would your life look like?

Notice how detailed it is.

In Charlie's words:

> *"I really wanted to get inside my readers' heads, just to make sure I had a deep understanding of what they most wanted."*

After Charlie got his *answer* regarding workaholics with anxiety problems, he used them as the *basis* of the back-cover copy. He formulated it using questions:

- Do you live in constant fear?

- Do you worry that something terrible is about to happen?
- Do you have trouble breathing, relaxing, and sleeping?
- Do you think you're losing control, and that you're going to die?
- Are you trapped in your own personal hell, and don't know how to get out?

You are going to model this, too.

Write Your Back Cover Copy

Find a book that is a bestseller. Find your favorite book. The one you love. Notice what about the back cover appealed to you. Then *model* the way they structure their message.

Typically, it will be about connecting to the audience, their experience, their problem, and then positioning the promise.

Write your draft. You can always refine and rewrite it later. But write it down now.

This is the *final copy* that Charlie used for the back of his book.

Notice how compelling it is for his target reader. You, too, should strive to have the similar results.

> *"I've been there, and I know what it's like. Shallow breathing, tension in the gut, chest pains, rapid heartbeat… Every moment is exhausting, crushing, and painful. Anxiety destroys your confidence, your productivity, your relationships, and your ability to enjoy life. The worst part is the obsessive hopelessness—the gnawing sense that you'll never feel happy again.*
>
> *Fear no more. You can put an end to your suffering. You can start living again. And it's not as hard as you think…"*

Play It Away covers my entire journey: what caused my anxiety, the "A-ha!" moment that lead to my cure and how I got my life back. In this book, you'll learn:

- *The key breakthrough that allowed me to enjoy life again (page 27)*
- *My step-by-step plan for healing anxiety without drugs (page 47)*
- *How I turned non-stop worrying into background noise (page 95)*
- *My unusual technique for stopping panic attacks (page 100)*
- *Why "anchors" fuel anxiety, and how to remove them (page 49)*
- *How I finally started sleeping well again (page 85)*
- *Three common nutrient deficiencies that amplify anxiety (page 114)*
- *How to boost productivity and have guilt-free fun (page 70)"*

The back-cover done right, makes the reader feel like the book was written *just for them*. And that by some *divine* power, they arrived at the answer to the question or problem that has been plaguing them for so long!

Write your titles, write your subtitles, get your cover designs drafted, and write the back-cover description.

Well, obviously you're going to deliver your content and tell your stories. But that's not all you want in your book.

Here are some pretty standard and generic sections:

- Title Page.
- Copyright Page.
- Free Bonus Page.
- Review Page.
- Dedication.
- Acknowledgements.
- Preface.
- Foreword.
- Introduction.
- About The Author.
- Products And Programs.
- Table of Contents.

You don't have to have _all_ of these, but you do get to choose which ones are right for your book. I will describe each, briefly below.

The title page of a book is the page at or near the front which displays its title that may be shorter than what's on the cover. It also may display the author and the imprint of the publisher. It's typically printed in a fashion that is similar to the rest of the text within the book.

It's one of the most important parts of the preliminary content of a book, as the information in it is typically used to establish the proper title proper and often the statement of data relating to publication.

The copyright page is usually on the back of the title page. It often contains a copyright notice, legal notices, disclaimers, publication information, current edition, printing history and an ISBN that uniquely identifies the book. It can also include bulk ordering information for the book, and contact information for the publisher.

The free bonus page is not a required page in your book, but it's an excellent idea to include a way for people to take a "next step" with you, BEFORE they ever even consume your content. (See the front of this book for an example.)

The review page is also not required, but is a great way to offer third-party credibility as to the value of your content. These are basically quotes and testimonials from people who have already read your book, and have high praise for it.

The acknowledgement page in a book is where the author thanks people who helped make the book possible. Acknowledgment pages are traditionally placed within the front matter of books, though they will occasionally appear in the back instead. (It is also sometimes grouped within the preface.)

If the acknowledgment section stands alone, however, it typically follows the preface. Alternatively, some authors choose to place the acknowledgments either before or after the table of contents. Discuss the placement with your editor to help select the best spot for your section.

An acknowledgment section might initially seem like the simplest part of writing your book, but many authors feel stumped once they reach this part of the publishing process.

How long should it be? Who should i thank? How should I say it? It can get surprisingly complicated surprisingly quickly.

Here are some tips to write a great book acknowledgment page:

1. **Who to thank:** Think about a wedding invitation list. If you've ever worked on one of those, you know the list can get pretty long once you start brainstorming and it can leave you overwhelmed with who to thank.

   A good rule of thumb is to stick only to the people who helped you directly in writing and producing the book (i.e.: not your friend from Pre-K who showed you how to tie your shoes—as invaluable that life lesson may be). Common acknowledgment ideas are family members, sources for nonfiction pieces, your editor and designer/illustrator, your publisher, and your book mentor.

2. **Length:** A short acknowledgement section is typically best, so try to keep it to one page. You shouldn't be afraid of offending anyone you leave out.

3. **Tone:** The tone of an acknowledgment page can be tricky.

   As a nonfiction author, you can write in a casual tone, but not stray too far from the tone used throughout your book. (Taking a look at other acknowledgment pages of comparable titles will go a long way.)

   Overall, the best way to write an acknowledgement is to make it personal, professionally casual, and descriptive. Don't simply say, "Thanks to my editor, Suzie." Instead, tell us why Suzie rocked. If you've written a fiction book, this could be the only place you get to write in your own voice instead of a characters', so make it count.

4. **Privacy:** As for me, I typically include anyone I want in this section without asking permission. (I've always been of the mind that I'd rather seek forgiveness than permission.)

However, you might consider asking permission of those you plan to include in this section before including them, especially if you're not close with them. This is especially relevant for nonfiction authors or authors whose books may be controversial; some interviewees you'd like to acknowledge may wish to remain undisclosed because of privacy issues. If you're not completely sure they're on board, it's always better to ask first than risk losing a supporter.

Overall, you should have a little fun with your acknowledgments, and definitely don't ignore them! This is a great opportunity to formally thank all of those who have helped you accomplish the amazing feat of publishing your book.

The about the author page is important.

Even though very few authors think about it, and even less write a good one, the "Author Bio" section of your book has impact. It will affect your sales, your reputation and it can even determine "if" and "what kind" of media you get.

Unless you're an author with household name (Steven King, JK Rowling, James Paterson), then you have to assume that most people who come across your book will not know who you are.

So how will they learn about you?

Regardless of if they learn about it from inside your book, on your website, on your Amazon page, or your marketing materials; *for most readers, your author bio is it.*

Again, this can dramatically impact your sales and reach directly.

If you can establish yourself as an authority about your book topic, readers will be much more inclined to buy your book, read it, and engage you beyond the book you the way you want them to. (i.e. buy your products and services)

People who are considering spending their disposable income on your book and your products and programs are looking for a reason to do it or not do it. A great bio helps them pull the trigger, while a bad bio can stop them cold.

Furthermore, if you want your book to help build your business, and establish your credibility and authority in a subject, often the author bio can actually be more important than what's actually in the book.

A sad but true reality is that more people will read your author bio than your actual book.

Think about it: It takes a long time to read a book. But, how easy is it to make a snap judgment based on a short paragraph that describes the author.

In a world where people are constantly bombarded with information, most people choose the latter.

This is doubly true for media.

Most people in media work very hard under tight deadlines, and don't have time to read long books or even long, meandering pitch emails. A good author bio cuts right to the point by saying: *this is someone who is important and I need to pay attention to them.*

How To Write Your Author Bio

Now I'll be the first to admit, that I went a little overboard on the author section of this book. For some reason, it felt called to share a bit more of my background and my struggles than I'd typically suggest adding to a book.

However, as you can see, it's 100 percent your choice. I felt like making mine long, and telling a bit about my story, and that's okay. (At least to me.)

Writing about yourself as an author is typically a task that most writers shy away from, but writing an effective author bio doesn't have to be so painful.

With a few simple tips you can have an effective bio that will hopefully impress interested readers and publishers, and also help you sell your books products and services.

First think, "less" is typically more when it comes to author bios, and you want to make sure you do (and don't do) the following:

1. Demonstrate your authority and credibility regarding your subject (but don't overstate it)

2. Include things that are interesting and build your credibility (without going overboard)

3. Mention your website and any books you have previously written (but don't oversell them)

4. Drop relevant names, if they are appropriate (without being crass about it)

5. Keep it short and interesting (without leaving things that are important out)

You notice a pattern here?

Good author bios walk the line between being ridiculously over-promotional and arrogant, and being boring and uninspiring.

While your readers are interested in finding out more about you, they don't want to get bored, or listen to arrogant braggadocio about how awesome you are. If your bio is too long, or too full of overstated accomplishments and awards, it will turn your readers off and actually make you look less credible. (Again, less is often more.)

A good rule of thumb is to keep your bio under 250 words.

Anything longer than that means you've gone on too long about your accomplishments, your personal life or both. Cut it down to the most important things.

(Or completely disregard my advice. As you can see from the long bio I added to this book, I included a significant amount of information about my personal life that I thought people might want to know.)

So it's up to you.

Your Bio Grows As You Grow

Your author bio as a living document. As you change and grow so too should your bio. Just because you've written it once, doesn't mean it's finished forever.

If you are writing for different genres or different topics, some of your accomplishments and past works will be more relevant to your readers than others. Typically, I suggest that you tweak your author bio for each new book you release.

If You Find This Difficult, Get Help

People, especially writers, have a hard time writing about themselves. Often, the Author Bio is the most difficult part of the marketing process.

If you are unsure about whether your author bio seems either incomplete, or too arrogant, run it by a few friends for feedback. It's often easier for someone else to praise you and see the amazing things you do—instead of you.

Take This Seriously

Getting your author bio "right" is an important task.

As I've already stated, this small section is often the ONLY source of information potential readers have about you (the author). That's one of the reasons "why" it's so important. And why it impacts your marketability and success of your book. Take it seriously, get it right, and it will help you build your brand, promote your books and grow your business.

What Goes Inside Your Book?

Here are some pretty standard and generic sections:

- Dedication.
- Preface.
- Foreword.
- Introduction.
- Table of Contents.

The dedication is typically an honoring of someone or a group of people to whom the book is dedicated. This is a very personal thing.

Some people choose grandparents, parents, and kin. Others choose the world, Mother Nature, or the next generation of children coming into the world.

There's no hard and fast rule. If you are unsure, *model* a bestselling book. Modeling is a concept we've already covered.

The preface is a short 1-2-page contribution by *someone else*, a *subject matter expert* who can testify to the importance of your book. Typically, this involves commenting on your (the author's) personality and why they chose to endorse the book. Though the preface *isn't* a <u>must-include</u>, it's a nice thing to have.

The *easiest* way to get your preface done is to ask someone who is credible to endorse your book with a preface. Tell them the title, subtitle, and what it is about. Show them the back-cover copy. And then ask them if they would be willing to write the preface to your book.

The foreword is a (usually short) piece of writing sometimes placed at the beginning of your book, typically written by someone other than the author. It often tells of some interaction between the writer of the foreword and the book's primary author or the story the book tells.

Oftentimes, they are written by someone well-known or famous to a particular audience or industry.

The introduction is an expanded version of your *back-cover copy*. Which is why it was so important to spend time on your cover, front and back.

The introduction, like the back cover, tells a bit about your story, builds credibility with you as an individual, and expands on the problem and promise you positioned in the back copy.

It also tells them *how* to go about getting the most out of this book. If you are unsure of the structure, *copy* the structure of the introduction to this book!

This is what my introduction did:

- Connected to the common problem people have when writing a book.
- Explained what the wrong book is.
- Explained what the right book is to grow your business.
- Explained why this book is so important.
- Communicated the results you can gain as a reader.

Model it!

Map out your table of contents

The main aspect of structuring the content of your book is the *table of contents*.

One way to look at it is as if it's a **Treasure Map**.

One that leads people through a journey that ultimately takes them to—*do what you want them to do.* (i.e., work with you, follow you, and buy your stuff.)

Consider: What do you want your reader to *get* by the time they finish your book? What do you want them to do *feel*? What do you want them to do *next*?

Hopefully, this is becoming more clear to you by now. If not, don't worry. You're not alone. That's why we're here to help you when you're ready.

I'll also structure a table of contents in a linear fashion. What needs to happen first? Second? Third? Etc.

Got it? Great.

Let's move on.

Now that you know where they need to be by the end of the book, and where they are *right* now; the table of contents is about the logical steps to get them from point A to Point B.

Point A is where they are now.

Point B is the *promised land*.

Point A is represented by where they are now:

- What are they thinking?
- What are their challenges?
- What are their hopes?
- What are their dreams?
- What do they want most?

Then Point B is about where they ought to end up:

- What is the new way of thinking?

- What did they get that they needed, but didn't think they did?

Then the table of contents is simply covering the first, second, third, etc. steps to get there. That is:

- What is the first step they need to take?
- What is the second step they need to take?
- What is the third step they need to take?

And so forth.

You can break it down even further with these bonus questions:

- What do they need to understand?
- What about their thinking needs to change first?
- What do you need to tell them first, so they change their thinking?

And so on.

If the subject was about having *cleaner, whiter, and stronger teeth*: the reader would need to pick up a brush, squirt toothpaste, brush with a circular technique, rinse their mouth with water, and floss regularly.

They would probably have to learn how to *select* a toothbrush that is an appropriate size and tension for them. And, they would probably need to be aware of how to floss without damaging their gums.

This is just to illustrate.

Model the same thinking to map out your table of contents.

<u>Here's an example.</u>

When I helped Steve Napolitan write his book *Capture Clients Close Deals*, I asked Steve, "What's the <u>first</u> thing you want your reader to do, to help them capture more clients and close more deals?"

His response, "*I want them to stop pitching and start giving.*"

Simple. And if you look inside his book, that's his *first chapter*. It's called "*Stop Pitching and Start Giving.*"

Basically, Steve wanted people to understand that sales isn't about asking people to buy your stuff (it's not pitching). He wanted people to understand that sales is about *giving first*. To be in *service*.

I then ask, "Okay, now they understand to stop pitching and start giving, what do they need to do next?"

He says, "They need to stop guessing and start knowing what clients want."

The next chapter became *Stop Guessing and Start Knowing*. Steve shares about how people need to stop guessing what their clients want and start knowing, by *surveying* them. They need to just *ask* their customers what they want.

You can do the same, too.

Keep doing this until you help the reader reach Point B, the promised land!

If you've not done so already,

Draft Your Table Of Contents Now.

You'll probably revise it multiple times, but it's important to get started. Once you start, all the steps become clearer and clearer. Organizing your content actually helps you better understand your own content.

Bake Marketing Into Your Book

Remember that your book is "bait."

Have you ever heard of a fisherman, coming home after a long day of fishing, excited to throw his unused worms into a frying pan to fry them up for supper?

Of course not. Your book is bait to "attract" your ideal perfect prospect. Once you've hooked them, wouldn't it be polite if you fed them something a little more substantial than worms?

Whatever that "next step" is, is what they really want and need. Your book is the beginning. Don't get confused that it's your main course. Your main course, are your products and programs that you strategically design to serve people who *want* your help, assistance, or guidance.

We like to say you *bake* some marketing into your book. Meaning you add in one ingredient at a time, that altogether bakes into something appetizing and delicious by the end of the book.

I know I keep repeating myself, but it's important to know what you're going to sell or offer, or where you can direct people to in your book.

Add Bonuses

You absolutely want to add bonuses to your book.

On the front of this book, I'm giving away a free Quick Start Audio training that helps people go from Blank Page to Bestseller in 90 days or less.

I direct people to go to my website TrevorCrane.com/freeaudio to give me their email address, in exchange for the audio training.

This allows me to *start* a relationship with my readers. They get to hear my voice. And when they opt-in, I get what marketers call *a new lead*.

Now, you can *always* add the bonus in your book more than once. Just as a reminder. Like how I mentioned it again in *this chapter*, even though my bonus offer is on the front cover of this book.

Also, in the front of my book, and the back of my book, I give away a free and more in-depth webinar training. I direct people to go to my website EpicAuthor.com/free to again give me their email address, in exchange for the training.

The bonus also doesn't have to be a free audio, or webinar or free ebook download.

For example:

T. Harv Ecker, author of *Secrets of the Millionaire Mind*, gives away *two free tickets* to his live event, worth $2,590.

People then go to his event, where he sells them other events, products and training programss.

Regularly, Mr. T. Harv Ecker would earn over $1 Million Dollars a weekend from his events. Often much more.

Consider what bonuses you might want to give away in your book, and how you might position them.

And if you don't know the answer now, that's okay, too. Add that to the list of things you still need to figure out. (I didn't know ANY of the answers to these questions when I got started.)

Just make sure there is a way for you to capture leads.

If they bought your book, they are receptive to buying other stuff you come out with. By capturing their email address, you can keep them updated on what you have on offer.

I recommend sending them to a "landing page" that collects their email address.

NOTE: In my Epic Author Academy program, I give my members access to the exact templates we use to set this all up, so you don't have to worry about it. It comes with a book website, and book sales funnels, etc.

"Seeding" Your Products and Services

Once you know what you're offering beyond your book, you can knowingly plant little "seeds" or stories, that ideally create a growing desire for people to want what you're offering.

I do that with a lot of stories.

I suggest that you do the same.

I'm sure you've noticed, that in this book, I've shared a lot of *stories* about the *successes* of my clients.

That wasn't by *accident*.

I also think it's a cool way to bring attention to them, instead of myself. I think it's much better received than out-and-out *bragging* about how "awesome" I am. But what you will find is that by lifting up other people, you're automatically raised along with them.

I do my best to <u>never</u> miss a chance to praise and compliment and promote my clients.

<u>Planting seeds can also mean asking the right questions.</u>

Some questions are designed to create a desired future-state, and to pique the reader's imagination and curiosity about having and living with the results they desire in the future. This creates a "pull" for the reader to want to have that *desired* state or awesomeness, more than their present state, of less than awesomeness.

We call this "the gap."

The questions you ask and the content you provide should be selected carefully, to try to elicit the emotion of the people you are communicating with, so that it grows and grows and grows until they can't take it anymore and…they hire you and buy your stuff.

Now, you might be thinking, "Oh, my God… *Is this manipulation?*

Yes.

You WANT to "manipulate" and "influence" and use every single weapon at your disposal to trick, cajole, and incentivize

people to do what you know in your <u>soul</u> will serve them at the highest level.

Look, I'm taking a wild guess here...

I'm assuming that you're not an asshole.

If you are, and you're really a bad person out there trying to do bad things, then you shouldn't be trying to persuade and influence people.

Shame on you then.

But I think I've really met more than 2-3 real assholes in my entire life.

Most people are good, and they're trying to do good.

I understand that there are bad people out there, and that bad things happen. But, my guess is you're not one of them.

I'm guessing you're powerfully awesome.

But, just like Stan Lee said through Spiderman,

"With great power, comes great responsibility."

You owe it to the world to get your message out there in every way you can.

If not, you're holding back your gifts, and everyone loses.

<u>**An example:**</u>

Throughout the book, I mentioned my Epic Author Academy and

Epic Author Mentoring programs.

These are programs where you get to plug into a community of business owners wanting to use a book to grow their business and get the mentoring and resources to make it happen.

Notice what I did there? Heh heh. Was that subtle? Maybe yes, maybe no. I don't know. I do the best I can. If people like it, cool. If not, oh well. I won't apologize for doing the best I can. And neither should you.

All I know is when I *seed* my services, it gives people a glimpse into a future where I can support them at a higher level. I do it to help people, to move past their excuses and their limitations, and beyond the patterns they've been running that are not helping them get to the next level.

You should, too.

Remember my story about Gennadi and Alla?

Well, in the book Alla purchased, I planted the seed that they could get *private coaching* with me. All they had to do was go to my website. There, I offered them a chance to set an appointment to get a complimentary call with me. They completed a short *survey*, and then boom, I got to decide if I wanted to work with them.

Notice what I did there? I didn't do a hard sell. I gave them an *invitation* to take the next step. There are many different types of calls-to-action.

It all depends on what you're offering.

You probably have small, medium, large and extra-large items for sale. So, just think of these as A, B, C, and D. Then choose the chapters where you want to *seed* your programs.

Another example.

Meet Eric

Eric Tomas is also known as ET, The Hip Hop Preacher.

I fell in LOVE with ET watching his YouTube videos. Man, the guy has great energy, he's passionate as hell and he is one of the most inspirational speakers I've ever met.

ET started giving away his "greatness" on YouTube for free.

Once he finally published his first book, I didn't just get the paperback version, I scooped up the audiobook. I listened to it twice.

About a year later he came out with his second book.

While I was buying his second book, he offered me the chance to get his workbook. I got that, too.

(The workbook, by the way, contained the same content that was inside the book. It just gave me space and pages to write my answers down.)

Now, you might think, "Hey! That bastard got twice the amount of money out of Trevor."

Yep.

But I didn't care.

I was happy. Thrilled even.

Eventually, I paid a bunch more to go to one of ET's "live events."

It was awesome.

Next?

ET offered me a monthly continuity program, where I can pay a monthly tuition ($49 to $199 a month) to be part of his „Breathe University."

(I didn't buy that yet, but I considered it.)

However, I'll probably buy more stuff from him in the future.

I'm happy. He's happy.

The reason I'm bringing all of this up, is that I'm happy to buy from someone I know, like and trust.

But if ET didn't give me anything else except his free videos, I'd have missed out on everything else he has to offer.

His books gave me a deeper insight into his character, and inspired me to want more of what he had to offer.

Thank God he gave me more options.

ET "seeds" his products and programs in his books, in his videos, in his emails and in all of his marketing.

I don't buy "everything" he offers and that's okay.

ET keeps adding more value, and keeps giving me new options to buy more products and services from him. (That's a GOOD thing.)

What's important here is for you to remember the IMPORTANCE of "seeding" things in your *book*, and your *videos*, and your *emails*, and your *marketing*.

Many people are "scared" to make offers to their clients, or followers, or readers. Don't be. You can't make everyone happy. Some people will like it, some people won't. Some people will buy it, some people wont.

Who do you want to focus on?

The people who want MORE of what you have to offer? Or the people who DON'T want more of you and what you have to offer?

As ET says,

> "Go where you're celebrated not tolerated."
> —ET, The Hip Hop Preacher

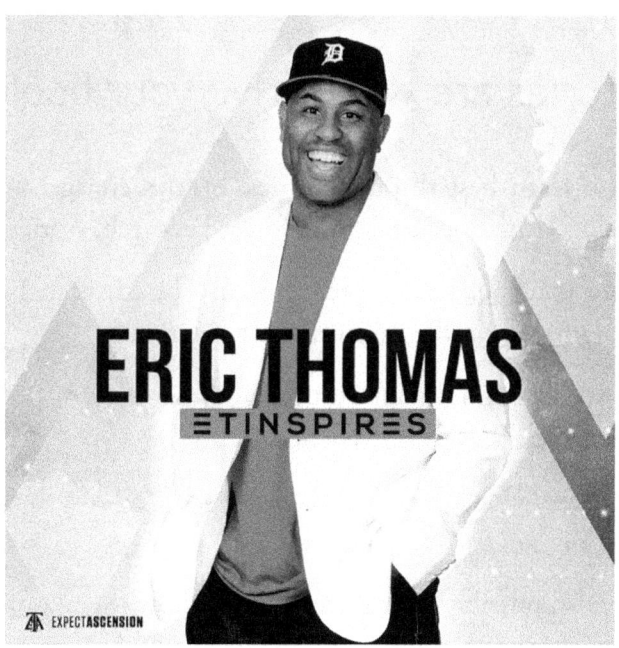

What stories should you share?

I know we've been talking a lot about stories, but let's just go a little further.

Now that you have a table of contents and main points that you want to communicate, you need to fill in the chapters with relevant and engaging content.

How do you do that?

Stories.

As I've shown in this book, you can share case studies, personal stories, stories about famous people.

You can, *and should*, reference famous people and popular movies.

Stories are what drive your book.

People also learn best through stories. Stories engage. Stories are memorable. Remember I said it before, "Facts tell, stories sell."

Sharing your personal experiences also builds your brand and trust through your authenticity and transparency.

Case studies show your reader proof of what is possible for them when they take your guidance.

Remember, you are trying to demonstrate how they can get from A to B.

You're also possibly telling stories that show them a future they desire. And stories that are warnings they should avoid.

Don't be afraid to give away your best stuff.

Example:

Let's say you're an expert at teaching people how to clean their teeth and save thousands of dollars in dental bills.

You could tell them a story about how you calculated the cost of *not* cleaning your teeth.

If they need to learn how to pick the right toothbrush, you can share a story about how *different* people have different gums and different sized mouths. And that the *right* toothbrush size is important, or you can't reach the "hard to clean spots."

This is just to illustrate. Notice it isn't about sharing *your whole life story*.

It's about staying relevant.

You don't want to "overpack their backpack." That'll just be exhausting and slow them down.

Give them just enough in each chapter, so they understand what you want to communicate, so they can successfully move on to the next step.

Within each chapter, the purpose of every paragraph is to get the reader to read the next paragraph. And so on.

Take a moment to think about *what's relevant* to share with your reader. What stories will help them get from Point A to Point B?

What do you need to tell them, so they read the next paragraph?

Again, we covered this in previous chapters, but it's about asking the right *questions*.

The right *questions* extract the most useful *answers*.

When we discussed the *table of contents*, remember the question, "What's the first thing you want the reader to do?" And for Steve, it was to *Stop Pitching and Start Giving*.

Don't know how to write a story?

No problem.

I'll give you a little insight here.

Here's where to get started:

1. Find stories you like. Stories that really stick with you. And model those.

2. Join our Epic Author Academy Community. Get a team. Someone there can teach you. Or better yet, as you will find out, someone can *write those stories* for you. (I talk about this in the Speak, Scribe, Source chapter of this book.)

Remember, you don't have to be the expert at everything.

Far from it.

Just do what you're good at, and find other people to do the rest.

Now that you understand the thinking involved, I'm going to show you the steps to help you write your book even faster than you thought.

Onward.

ACTION STEP

Action Step

Write down at least 10 titles.

_____
_____
_____

Write down at least 10 subtitles.

_____
_____
_____

Write a short description of your book.

_____
_____
_____

List 5 possible bonuses you could offer in your book.

_____
_____
_____

List what products or services you could offer beyond your book.

_____
_____
_____

SIX
Set A Date

"Real artists ship."
—**Steve Jobs**

There's nothing like a <u>deadline</u> to help you get something done.

I honestly don't think I *ever* would have gotten *any* of my books done, unless I'd had a deadline when the book was due.

Somehow, something just always seems to get in the way, until…I have no choice left but to make it "good enough" and get it out there.

This is one of the reasons that I love, love, LOVE the pre-launch partnership that's available to us through Amazon and KDP (Kindle Direct Publishing.)

I'll discuss this more in Chapter 10, but in essence, they give you 90 days from the day you load your book on their site, to get your book done.

This means you can pre-launch, or pre-sell your book. BEFORE it's done.

Setting a date helps you get your book done fast.

According to Parkinson's Law: "Work expands so as to fill the time available for its completion."

Another way of saying it is that, *things typically take as much time as you give them.*

Besides, now, this should be easy for you, because, now you know what's involved. *Okay, granted, you probably don't have all the details yet, and you're only in Chapter Five of this book, but theoretically, the next step for you, once you do have clarity, is to set a due date.*

Again, I suggest that first you know the *path*, and steps or the "strategy" you will implement, PLUS I hope you understand the "structure" of the content for your book.

But once you've got that, it's time to set a clear and realistic date for your book's release.

If you don't set a date, it won't get done.

Period.

I'm not sure you read the Steve Jobs quote at the beginning of this chapter, "Real artists ship." What Jobs meant was that at some time you have to DECIDE "when" you're going to deliver your product to your customers.

Your product, in this case, your book, doesn't do anyone any good unless you get it into their hands.

Perfection Is Your Enemy

A teacher of mine once asked me, "What are the lowest expectations you can have for yourself?" I hesitated, slightly confused, then mumbled a guess: "I don't know… low expectations? I guess? No expectations? Failure?"

He said, "Perfection."

It hit me like a ton of bricks.

I had to let it marinate to understand his answer. Here's the deal. Perfection doesn't exist. When you expect it, you immediately set yourself up for failure.

Why?

Because you've set an <u>unattainable</u> standard for yourself that can never be reached.

People do this all the time, unknowingly setting the *lowest* expectation for themselves, disguised by mistakenly thinking it is the highest.

Instead of making your book a perfect representation of your heart and soul, and making sure that it has every single story that's ever happened to you from birth, (we talked about what stories you should use in Chapter 4), *let your book be great*, and get it out there.

(Granted, if you've been plagued with perfectionism in the past, this might mean "good-enough" in your mind, but don't apologize for it, or delay it. Get it done.)

Contrary to popular belief, "perfection" is not the highest standard, it's the lowest.

Yes, make it great.

But don't try to make it perfect.

ACTION STEP

Nothing motivates people more than a deadline.

When you set a date, your brain instantly starts to figure out what needs to be done, by when, etc.

Pull out your calendar, and pick a "shipping" date when you'd like to have your book done.

For right now, don't worry about whether or not it's the *perfect* date.

In Chapter 10, we'll discuss more about the strategy of using Amazon and KDP as your partners to help you schedule a pre-launch of your book.

NOTE: It's not until you first upload your book to KDP, that the date is set in stone.

But, more about that later.

For now, enter the date you selected below.

By when would you like to be an author, or publish your next book?

Set A Date:

PRODUCE

*"The best way to get your book written fast
is to set a date it's getting done."*
—**Trevor Crane**

SEVEN
Speak, Scribe, Source

"I have told people that writing this book has been like brushing away dirt from a fossil. What a load of shit. It has been like hacking away at a freezer with a screwdriver."
—**Amy Poehler**

It's time to "produce" your book.

<u>Notice, I did not say "write."</u>

Of course, you can *write* your book the old fashioned way, but in this chapter we're going to talk about a nice 3-step process that can help you capture your ideas quickly, and can often get your first draft done, or possibly the foundation of your book done, *"Faster than you can say, 'Bob's your uncle?!'"*

By the time you reach this stage of the process, you should have a very good idea of the answers to the four questions we asked in Chapter 5.

Here they are again:

- Who you are writing your book for?

- What is your book about?
- Why do they care? (Problems and results.)
- What do you want them to do next?

Asking and answering these is REALLY important.

Most people don't take the time to get this type of clarity.

Then, their book sounds like they're speaking Chinese to an English-speaking audience.

If you now have "clarity" about WHO your book is targeting, you're on the right track! (If you don't have clarity yet, go back and do the exercises to help you get that clarity.)

With this clarity, you know who your audience is, their challenges, their hopes and dreams, and where you want them to go—*next*.

Reminder: "next" refers to the CTA, or call-to-action, that you give them if you want them to work with you 1-on-1, or buy your products and services, etc. So, this also assumes that you understand *what* you are selling them, or pointing them to, beyond your book.

At this point, you should also understand the *structure* and *content* outline for your book, as it addresses the problems they might be struggling with, and the results they want to have.

If you're with me so far, then you're ready!

Let's start getting your book done!

As I said, before, this is a step-by-step process.

Step 5: Speak,

Step 6: Scribe, and

Step 7: Source.

This will be especially helpful to you, if you don't consider yourself a writer, or don't have time to write.

Or, if you just don't want to sit down with a pencil, or at your computer and peck away at the keyboard.

Not a problem.

You can *still* get your book done.

In fact, as far as I know, these three methods are the only ways to get your book done: Speak, Scribe or Source.

(I'll explain these in more details in a minute. But my perferred way of getting my books done, is to use all three. I'll explain.)

You can choose any one of these three methods.

Or, use a combination of all three. I use a combination.

As I said, here are the three steps: **Speak. Scribe. Source.**

(See Figure 2: Perform—as a little checklist to help you.)

SEVEN - SPEAK, SCRIBE, SOURCE

SPEAK/SCRIBE/SOURCE:

How are you going to write your book?
(Speak, Scribe, Source? Or all three?)

1. SPEAK
If you choose to "preform" your book, pick which of the following is your preferred method to get your content created.

✱ Teach:

   ▪ tele-class
   ▪ webinar
   ▪ live event
   ▪ course

✱ Interview:

   ▪ You interview people
   ▪ Someone interviews you

✱ Video:

   ▪ For Youtube or Facebook?
   ▪ For a Product?
   ▪ For a Podcast?

✱ Use as a Bonus?

   ▪ Yes
   ▪ No

✱ Record on your Phone:

   ▪ Use your voice recorder
   ▪ Free Conferencing
   ▪ _____

✱ Other:

   ▪ Dragon Dictate
   ▪ Google Voice
   ▪ Evernote
   ▪ _____
   ▪ _____

2. SCRIBE
Who will you get to HELP YOU "write" your book?

   ▪ You?
   ▪ Transcription _____ _____
   ▪ Ghost Writer _____ _____

3. SOURCE
   ▪ Content _____ _____
   ▪ Grammer _____ _____
   ▪ Formatting _____ _____
   ▪ #1 status.

Figure 2 - PERFORM

Speak It

At the risk of sounding overly simplistic, and redundant, instead of writing your book, you can speak it instead.

Now whether you choose to talk into a microphone or webcam, or your phone, or video camera, or whatever…all you are really doing here is sharing your knowledge, and quite likely talking about what you're already great at, and are probably talking about every day already.

When I work with my clients to help them plan a strategy to speak their book, I try to help them get creative and use something I like to call NET time. Or, "No Extra Time."

This way, we can leverage something else they are already doing, into getting out the content for their book. This could be previously scheduled speaking engagements, or webinars, or regular meetings with staff, etc.

And, I like to use a vehicle in which we can increase their exposure and broadcast their message to more people, i.e., *marketing*.

For example,:

I have used podcast episodes to help me, or my clients extract the content. We've offered special webinars or tele-classes that promise to teach the content that will go in their new upcoming book.

Here's an example:

> In the introduction of this book, I told a story about Steve Napolitan.
>
> Steve got his book written quickly using this strategy.

To pick back up on that story, once we got clarity about the four questions gave you, (Who? What? Why? and What's next?), Steve chose to teach a six-module tele-class to rip his content.

To help make sure Steve got it done quickly, and didn't procrastinate, or overcomplicate things, I advised that he offer the tele-class to his existing list, *free of charge*.

This accomplished several things at once.

First, Steve created an incredible amount of goodwill with his audience, for offering such phenomenal value free of charge.

Second, this built some buzz and created some effective marketing for Steve, which built anticipation for his upcoming book.

Third, this ensured that Steve would keep his commitment because he had made a promise to his list, that he would show up and deliver great value.

Fourth, because Steve is an excellent trainer and coach, he now had a LIVE audience to connect with and assist, which is what he's great at anyway.

Fifth, Steve was efficient with his time, because he had to deliver the content within a set and scheduled period of time. In addition, this strategy cut out any analyzing and perfectionism from getting in the way of completing the content. (Oftentimes, when people record by themselves, they'll stop and start, and start over. But if you're LIVE, you don't have that choice.)

Sixth, Steve got nearly his entire book done on six simple calls, and less than a week of "work."

Seventh, Steve loves training and teaching, so it was bliss for him to capture his content this way.

Eighth, in thinking about how he could provide the most value to his audience in this fashion, he streamlined his content into comprehensive chunks that delivered the value he needed to deliver, but no more.

Ninth, offering this tele-class, helped Steve attract new clients into his speaking, coaching, consulting, and events.

Tenth, Steve now had an extremely valuable "program" that he chose to repurpose and now sells independently on his website as a $2,500 product.

How cool would that be?!

Would you like to create a $2,500 course while you create the content for your book?

I could go on, but this is just what comes to mind, off the top of my head.

Are you starting to see the possibilities, and the possible benefits for you, your book, and business?

Want another example?

My wife, Robyn, and I recently hosted a 2-day event we offer to our private clients called, Advanced Sales Mastery.

In preparation for her new book, Robyn selected the stories that she shared, and some of the content she delivered, so it could be repurposed for her new book.

Another option you could choose is to be interviewed by a peer or a friend.

Call them on a recorded phone line, and voila!

(If you like you can use a free service to do this like: FreeConferenceCall.com)

My 9-year-old daughter, Phoenix, is an author.

She speaks her stories into my iPhone, or I take a video of her telling the story for her books.

Her first book is now a series called, *The 3 Ninja Kitties.*

To create "this" book, I taught a special webinar to pull out new and relevant content that I could use for the book.

On that webinar, I taught some of the exact same content I'm sharing with you in this book.

For many people, I think this is an excellent choice to help you start the first draft of your book.

Why?

I know my stuff.

Steve knows his stuff.

My daughter knows her story.

And you know what you're best at.

Does this take a little preparation?

Does it take a little forethought?

Does it take a little work?

Of course.

Or else, every monkey would have a book.

And by the way,

I'm in no way saying this is <u>easy</u>.

It isn't.

It's *simple*. But it's not *easy*.

It's hard work.

Organizing your ideas in such a way that people understand them, and in an engaging way, is an art and a science.

Many people screw this up. Many people do this wrong. Many people create crappy books.

BUT NOT YOU, MY BROTHA! NOT YOU, MY SISTA!

You've got the hook-up. You've got this book.

You've got access to the free content and training that I give away on my website.

And you can get some help.

You can do this. But don't feel like you have to do this alone. That's foolishness.

<u>Want to know a little secret?</u>

This book is a result of webinars and videos I have done in the past. Shhh...don't tell anyone.

I created the outline, and I repurposed a bunch of my existing content. Then, I edited and organized it. YES, I'm TYPING these words right now.

But that's "editing."

That's me IMPROVING my content.

But the bulk of this book, came from me speaking it out loud into some sort of recording device.

Why else is speaking it out beneficial?

Because unless you are trained writer or copywriter, it's unlikely that you are going to write the way you talk. Oftentimes, the easiest way for a reader to *process* what you're saying, is to have your book written as if you are speaking to them face to face.

Just like this. When you're speaking to another human, it can be effortless.

In addition, planning out your table of contents and the outline of what people need to know so they can understand your book, and get massive value from your communication, makes organizing your content and the stories super simple.

How should you record yourself?

Goodness.

Yes.

Use anything.

Use everything.

Seriously.

Start with your phone.

Or video camera.

Or FreeConferencing.com, or Skype, or Zoom, or Dragon Dictate, or Google Voice, or Google Hangouts, or Facebook Live, or a Webinar, or Tele-class, or YouTube Live, or call your mother-in-law and leave a really long message on her old answering machine that's still sitting on her kitchen counter.

But do it.

Scribe It

There are two possible meanings in this segment or step.

First: I just mean that you transcribe your recordings. I like to use [rev.com](rev.com). They only charge $1.00 per minute, and they have a pretty good turnaround time, sometimes, less than 24 hours. They accept audio recordings and video files, and you can upload them, or use a link to files that already exist online.

Once they complete your word-for-word transcript, it's sent to you in a Word document.

Boom! First draft of your book—done.

Second: You scribe it or WRITE it out yourself.

Some people like to write.

My father-in-law likes to write and is currently writing his memoirs. He doesn't want to speak out his stories. The process of writing it all down is enjoyable for him. So, he's just writing it out.

As I edit this document this second, I'm "scribing." There, I just wrote that word. And this one. And this one as well. Nothing fancy.

However you slice it, at one stage or another, you, or someone, is going to have to look at the words that are on your page, and move them around a little bit, so they intrigue and engage your reader.

It makes sense right?

After it's transcribed, you need to have it properly organized, so it reads like a book, versus just an interview or random trainings.

Source It

I highly recommend this step.

Simply put, this means: GET HELP.

I hired a writer to help me write this book.

He spoke with me about the book first.

We worked together to organize my table of contents.

Then, he helped me take my transcripts and stories and turn them into magic. *(Is this magic? I hope so.)*

But you can also hire someone to do MOST of or ALL of the *writing* for you.

Sourcing it could mean that you hire a *ghostwriter* who interviews you, and pulls your content out of you, and turns it into amazing text.

I'll use Steve as an example again.

When Steve was putting his book together, he hired one of the writers we have on our Epic Author Publishing Team, who is also a friend of Steve's named, Jon Low.

What did Steve do while Jon was helping him with his book?

Well, he focused on what Steve did best; he went out and captured clients and closed deals.

He was earning money while his book was written for him!

(That's the name of his book, by the way, *Capture Clients Close Deals*.)

Now, Jon was a little more expensive than your basic writer, but he's an *amazing* writer.

But, Steve didn't mind investing in Jon, because with our guidance, Steve had happily made much more money than he'd invested, by merely marketing and promoting his book in advance of its release.

Also, Steve already had his table of contents laid out, and Jon Low knows our system. So, they got his whole book done in only 10 days!

Want to know who's helping me write this book? Mr. Jon Low. (aka "Badass" I wrote that part, not Jon.)

But understand me, every single word in this book is <u>mine</u>.

It's okay to get help putting your thoughts together. It's okay to have someone correct your language or grammar.

Get help. It's okay.

<u>What else should you get help with?</u>

Sourcing it is all about transforming your manuscript into your book.

In Chapter 8, I'll talk about the people I suggest you hire to help you build your publishing team, but for right now, imagine getting help from people who:

- Edit the _content._
- Check for _spelling_ and _grammatical_ errors.
- _Format_ your book so it can be _published._
- Get help to _promote your book to become a #1 bestseller._

Imagine you were building a house.

Would you go build it by yourself?

Or would you get some help?

Likely, you would _need_ to get some help.

You would hire an architect, builders, electricians, plumbers, painters, roofers, someone to install the carpet, someone to do the tile, someone to do the concrete work, etc.

Or maybe, you'd hire just one guy, or one company, to handle the whole thing.

Luckily, writing a book to build your business is a _little less complex_ than building a house.

In Epic Author Academy, I make these resources available to you, so you don't have to go search for them all on your own.

Over the last few years, I've accumulated the top people for my publishing team, that I now offer to you, _to help you get your book done._

Now, my clients and our community have the access I wish I'd had when I was first trying to get my book done.

If you want to do it fast, trust me, this is the way.

Most people think they need to write a book by themselves. *Nothing could be further from the truth.*

In fact, not even *famous* authors get it done alone.

They often have a coach, and editor, and a proofreader. They have people who *critique* their story and offer up *better suggestions*.

That's right. Think of any great book, and you will realize, there was a *team* behind it, that helped make it great.

But again… don't get caught up on needing to make it "perfect."

You Can Always Improve It In The Future

Other than *overwhelm*, and lack of *clarity*, it seems the one thing that seems to keep people from finishing their book, is their **addiction to perfection**.

Yes, I covered this a bit in the last chapter, but I want to talk about it again here.

One of the great things about the world we live in today is how awesome our technology is.

The world has truly changed.

No longer do you need some long, arduous process to edit your book.

Even after you formally "publish" your book, and make it available to the public, you can change anything about your book, and the changes will be reflected within 24-48 hours.

This means that when your mother-in-law finds a *typo* that you or your team missed, on Page 7...

Then, you (or someone on your team) can make the change, upload the new file, and you can ship your mother-in-law a new book.

"Freeeee... of Page-7 typos." (Say that like an evangelist preacher would say it - and it's more fun.)

You can even include with it a nice box of her favorite chocolates, all right from Amazon. If you have Amazon Prime, you might even be able to send it with FREE Shipping to boot!

Or better, you can have Amaon *gift* wrap it, and send her a *personalized* message on the card,

"Dear Mom: The weather is here, wish you were beautiful."

My point is, "You can make it better later."

You can always make a change or improvement, and I promise you, there will be typos, and updates you'll want to include; well, it can be done.

And on Amazon (where I recommend you first self-publish your book), you can have these changes made within minutes.

Yes, you can even include a cover design change, too.

Oh no!

Worried about "changing" your cover?

Well, look up the world famous, *Think and Grow Rich* book

online. It's probably one of the best self-help books of all time, and it has about 80 different colors and variations. (Mind you, you only need one for your book. Don't get confused.)

I'll say it again, in case you may have missed it:

In the digital world we are living in, if you want to change anything, you can *upload* the new version of the (word document, image, cover design, etc.), and it's almost instantly available!

It's that simple.

So, changes *after* you have finished your book are fine.

Improvements over time, are nothing you need to apologize for, they are called *improvements.*

They are somethign to be CELEBRATED.

Waiting for things to be *perfect* before you finish your book is a *disaster*.

That's called stagnation, procrastination, fear and failure.

Trust me. I've been there.

It stinks.

Follow the system.

Step by step.

Simple.

ACTION STEP

How will you "write" your book?

Speak:

What will you use to capture the meat of your book? (Webinar? Tele-Class? Recording Device? Trainings?)

_____

_____

_____

Scribe:

Will you transcribe audio/video files? Write your words? Or both?

_____

_____

_____

Source:

Who will help you write and edit your book?

Ghostwriter:

Editor:

Other:

EIGHT
Build Your Publishing Team

*"I am a member of a team, and I rely on the team.
I defer to it and sacrifice for it, because the team, not the individual,
is the ultimate champion."*
—**Mia Hamm**

By now you know that if you want to write your book to grow your business and do it fast, you can't do it alone.

But two things must be considered here. Especially when partnering up with service providers to get your book done:

1. **How much TIME does it take?**

Suppose you set a deadline to get your book done. Each component of producing a book takes time. And whether you are working on one aspect, or teaming up with someone to do it, you must know what the time constraints are.

2. **How much MONEY will it cost?**

There is a trade-off here. If it costs you more to do it yourself, then you shouldn't. So, you have to price how valuable your time is. If you spend one hour working on something you aren't good at and you don't want to do, what opportunity to earn money are you missing out on?

Everyone has different preferences.

It all depends on how quickly you want it done, and how much money and resources you are willing to invest to finish your book.

In my Epic Author Mentoring program, every member gets assigned a *project manager* to help them track and manage progress against a timeline.

That means; WHAT needs to get done, WHO needs to do it, WHEN it needs to get done, and HOW MUCH MONEY will be involved.

Additionally, we help you identify ways to get it done *fast* so that the *returns* exceed your cost of investment.

There are 5 people you need on your publishing team.

One caveat: these are the people I suggest you add to your team. If you already have someone who does one or more of the things for you below, then that's one less thing for you to worry about.

Note: You can also do it all yourself.

You can pay for it to be done. Or you can barter and have a friend or family member assist you. It's all up to you.

I just believe time is money, so even if you get it done for free, there is still a cost.

The following estimates are based on the assumption that you hire each of these team members on your own. When clients work with our team and use our shortcuts, they actually get a tremendous discount and learn ways to get great results from using our vetted vendors who give high-quality value for much less money and significantly less effort.

Of course, you can try to save money and skimp by not hiring all of these people on your team (or by hiring a low-quality team), but it could definitely cost you more time and money in the long run.

1. **DESIGNER** - The designer is one of the first people I hire when I'm working on a book. They'll create your book cover and any other artwork you need.

   You budget: **$1,000-5,000**.

   The reason I'm saying it's a grand to five grand is because it can be a real pain to find the right designer to do your cover, and some people will end up going back and forth through several designs to get it right (which can add up).

2. **WRITER** - You need a writer. You can write your own book. But you shouldn't have to do it alone. Ideally, find a professional writer. Someone who understands your tone and your voice who can make sure your message in your book is spot on.

   We covered this in previous chapters, but that includes; understanding the audience, baking the marketing into the book, and using engaging language to *compel* them to keep reading.

   A decent writer can cost anywhere between **$1,000-$5,000**.

   And remember, you could ask someone who is non-professional. A friend, your cousin, or spouse. This can make it cheaper.

But again, the time to get it done may well be more costly. Every moment you *don't* have your book to grow your business, you are *missing out* on more leads and clients! It's already costing you!

3. **EDITOR** - The third person you need is an editor. The editor and the writer are two different people.

   The editor is someone who makes sure you "dot your i's, and cross your t's." You don't want to skip this step. An editor adds that *extra touch* of professionalism.

   An editor will help you see what you may have missed. It's hard to see this for yourself. It's like looking behind your eyes.

   Ideally, you get a professional. You want to set aside anywhere between **$1,000-$5,000**. The price will depend on your deadline (how fast you want it done), and how much you are willing to invest.

4. **FORMATTER** - The fourth person you need, is someone to format your book. What is formatting? It is the *presentation* and *layout* of your text inside the book. Including: font, chapter headings, images, page size, etc.

   Your book has to be available in different formats for different platforms and media; online e-version, and offline print person. For example; Amazon, Amazon Kindle, Barnes & Noble, iBooks, and other bookstores.

   Your formatter ensures your book can fit on a number of these distribution platforms.

   You want to set aside anywhere between **$1,000-$5,000**.

5. **PUBLISHER** - The last person you need is a publisher. They will take your formatted manuscript, and publish it on

the relevant platforms.

If there was just ONE platform that is a MUST for your book to be on, it would be AMAZON.

You can try figuring this out all on your own. But it'll be time-consuming and involve lots of administration.

For example, you will need to create an ISBN number, select genres and categories for your book, register your keywords for the book, create an author profile, select pricing, fill out forms online, etc.

To do this yourself properly will take about two weeks. It is just easier to hire someone to get it done. Set aside about **$1,000-$5,000** to get someone to publish it for you.

If you do the math, that can cost about **$5,000-$15,000** to get your book done.

And that's assuming you get the *right* people on your team who will complete the tasks properly.

But, I have another option for you.

If you want use my team... I've taken care of all of this for you.

Not only will you save money, but you'll save something even more important - TIME.

Trust me, it took a lot of time and cost a bunch of money to find the *right* people for our team, and to have the *right* systems in place.

But now we have it down pat.

But for those of you who want to find and grow your team yourself, here is where I'd suggest you start looking:

1. **Design** - Fiverr.com, UpWork.com, 99Designs.com, Epic

Author Publishing & our Epic Author Team

2. **Write** - Upwork: Content, Epic Author Publishing & our Epic Author Team

3. **Edit** - Fiverr.com, Upwork: Content, Grammer.com, Epic Author Publishing

4. **Format** - Fiverr, Upwork, Epic Author Publishing & our Epic Author Team

5. **Publish** - UpWork.com, FreeLancer.com, Fiverr.com, Epic Author Publishing & our Epic Author Team

To save you the hassle and heartache of wasting time and money on the wrong person, members of the Epic Author Academy and Epic Author Mentoring Programs get access to our publishing team.

These are all people I have personally interviewed, tested, trained or worked with to ensure their quality, timeliness, and value for money. (**Aka: their awesomeness.**)

Our publishing team helps people in all stages of the writing, publishing and marketing phases of the process.

Because our process is so streamlined, our clients typically pay a fractionof the price that it would normally cost to get the help they need for thier book.

In addition, they stay *sane*, instead of having to figure it out themselves.

But, however, you go about doing it...

GET HELP.

Don't go it alone.

PUBLISH

"Take a look at what everyone else in your industry is doing, then do the complete opposite. You'll probably be very successful.
—**Dan Kennedy**

NINE
Self-Publishing vs. Traditional Publishing

"The journey of a thousand miles begins with one step."
—**Lao Tzu**

First off, what does it mean to "publish" your book?

Because, it can be kind of confusing

<u>Here's the definition of publish:</u>

"pub·lish"
to make it generally known, or make a public announcement
of your work being released for distribution

That's it.

So this means that if you start *"telling"* people about your book, to make it *"generally known"* …you're publishing.

Definitely, if they can get it from you, in ANY form, ebook, digital, audio, anything…you're publishing.

Now, my guess is you probably want a little bit more information than that, but before we move on to the details, I want you to notice something.

Please pay attention to the FIRST part of the definition, where it says you are *"publishing"* when you *"make it generally known."*

I think this is important because typically I work with business owners, speakers, coaches, and consultants, who have the challenge of getting leads, growing their income, raising their fees, booking speaking gigs, etc.

What I do is help them write a great book <u>fast</u>, and turn it into their <u>most powerful marketing tool</u>.

This helps them build their ideal business, so they can have the <u>time</u> freedom and <u>money</u> freedom that allows them to spend more time on what's most important to them.

Why do I bring this up?

Because "publishing" actually STARTS with "marketing."

What does that mean?

It <u>starts</u> when you start *telling* people about your book…even, and especially BEFORE it's even done.

Remember in Chapter 3, where we talked about how you should *"Tell The World?"*

Boom!

You want people to get *excited* about your book.

And this helps you get (and stay) excited about your book. And when you're talking to people about it, they tend to get curious, and then interested, and then:

1. You learn something about them, and what they like, and maybe you use that to change what you add to your book.

2. Everyone you talk to is a potential person who will buy and read your book.

So actually, "talking" about your book...

Throughout, EVERY phase and stage of its creation, INCLUDING THIS VERY SECOND THAT YOU ARE READING THESE WORDS, is one of the best and most powerful things you can do.

This chapter is about publishing, printing, and profiting from your new book.

I say, let's make that happen as soon as possible.

Billion dollar companies to it. Why can't you?

The "big boys" tell you about products and services that are not available yet... but will be *coming soon...* all the time.

I say, let's model them.

Now...

Traditional or Self-Publishing?

First, I'm the first to tell you that there's a place for both.

And I work with both traditional and self-published authors.

But if a new author comes to me, and they ask this question, the fastest answer for 98 percent of people is that you should self-publish. At least at first.

Let's not beat around the bush.

I could talk about this subject for pages and pages and pages… *or I could give it to you short and sweet.*

Now, if you're still wondering "why" I say this, then I'll share a few of my reasons below.

Yes, there is a time, and there is a place for going the traditional publishing route, I'm just saying that for most people, self-publishing is a good first choice.

Reasons why?

As you may already know, **it can take years to get published in the traditional way, and many never get published at all.**

So, why not self-publish now and keep ownership of your own book, and not give it away to someone else? When you go with a traditional publisher, they own your book. It's theirs.

Much of your control on your project is gone.

Another really good reason to self-publish now is that you can always go with a traditional publisher later. In all likelihood, you'll want to write another book, a better book, anyway. (I believe that you and your books, will get better and better.)

And when you do a good job promoting and profiting from your first book(s), once you finally crack-the-code, publishers will be chomping at the bit to work with you.

However, I want to say this as well:

There is no single right answer.

The world has dramatically changed.

Some self-published authors accuse traditionally-published authors of being misguided or short-sighted in their allegiance to a system that seems archaic and broken.

But there is no single right answer because it's context dependent.

This means the right answer can change—even for the same author—even from book to book, or from year to year.

However, there is a more important, and more relevant part of the question, that's rarely brought up around the topic of traditional vs. self-publishing, and it is about the RESULT you want, once your book is complete.

What result do you want?

My take is that REGARDLESS of "how" you publish, or "when" you publish… the most powerful thing for you to focus on is "marketing" your book.

And ideally, you use marketing strategies that build your business, your brand, your mission, your legacy and your bottom line.

<u>Start now.</u>

Not later.

Now.

Whether or not you choose to publish this way or that way… the MARKETING of your book is YOUR responsibility.

No one is going to tell the world about your book unless they have a reason to.

Your job is to find out what those reasons are, and get them talking about you, and your book NOW.

At the bare minimum, tell people you're writing a book about XYZ subject. Minimum.

If you were my client, I'd tell you to do a whole bunch more, but for starters, begin here.

"Hello world, I'm writing a book about _____."

If you have a sales process, and proven sales system in place, those new eyeballs, and new attention that you get just from "saying" you're writing a book, should turn into profit.

After that happens, you can call me up, and we can re-invest that into "you," and your business will really start blowing up.

(Or, if you don't convert any new clients, you may want to reach out to me even sooner, so I can help you switch that around.)

Oftentimes people are really close. They might just be a simple button-push away from total freedom and success, but they just need a little help figuring it out.

It's all good. We all need that help.

Are you *still* wondering if you should self-publish or traditionally publish?

You're not alone.

The same question is on the minds of many writers I meet, regardless of their career path or how established they are.

As I stated before: each author is different, *and each book is different*.

If you know your target market and have a clear set of goals for your book, you should be able to figure out the right publishing strategy for you.

One thing is certain: DON'T WAIT.

Start now.

Let this be the year you finally publish your book.

ACTION STEP

Who will be on your team, or what resources will you use to get your book done?

1. Designer
2. Writer
3. Editor
4. Formatter
5. Publisher

_____

_____

_____

TEN
Pre-Launch

"I think it is possible for ordinary people to choose to be extraordinary."
—**Elon Musk**

Pre-launching means that you put a product up for sale before it's actually available.

This means that people have the opportunity to purchase it before it's completed (or even created).

I talk to people every day who are uncomfortable with "selling" something that they haven't created yet. They often tell me that, "It just doesn't seem right."

But what you'll begin to notice, is that pre-launches are happening all the time.

Meet Elon

In April of 2016, hundreds of Tesla fans lined up outside dealerships to pre-order the new Model 3 sedan, before the car had even officially been unveiled.

Within the first week, Tesla CEO, Elon Musk, received almost

325,000 pre-orders, more than two times what they expected. In less than a month, Musk told reporters, "We are now almost at 400,000 orders for the Model 3…it surprised even us." With pricing starting at $35,000, Musk expects the Model 3 to reach in excess of 500,000 pre-orders before the first car is ever delivered.

Question:

Do you know how much 400,000 pre-orders times a $1,000 deposit is?

I'm not going to do the math for you. You should do it yourself—*and count the zeros.*

Actually, I take that back… I will do the math for you, just in case you miss it. It's $400,000,000 ($400 MILLION).

And that's just the deposit.

Take a lesson from the big boys. If you're "uncomfortable" selling something that doesn't exist yet, then it's time to pull up your panties and—***do it anyway.***

What's a pre-launch for your book?

Let's keep this really simple:

A pre-launch is making your book available for <u>*purchase*</u> before it's available for <u>*delivery*</u>. Fortunately for us, we get to do that using KDP, also called Kindle Direct Publishing.

It's a series of events that you set up to increase your exposure, credibility and even domination of a particular target market. Since your goal is to grow and expand your business, you want to take every opportunity you can to get attention and attract new customers.

Plus, you don't even have to have your book done *(or even started)* before you launch. What this allows you to do is elevate your positioning, authority, and status, right away.

It creates a buzz and gets people excited about your book. And if you take advantage of your pre-launch correctly, you can market it like crazy and put more money in your pocket.

Pre-launching a book on KDP is quite simple.

Meet Terrie

Terrie Matz, also known as TerriePathic, is an Animal Communicator and Reiki Practioner. When Terrie and I first started talking about her book, she had a pretty sizable challenge. Terrie couldn't see how it was appropriate for her to write a book, when she was relatively new to her field and had only just completed her certification.

She said something like this to me, "Trevor, how can I possibly be considered an expert, or write a book? I'm only just getting started. Who would want to listen to me?"

What Terrie didn't know, but completely embraced, when I brought it up as an option for her, was to write her book by becoming a "Research Expert."

What are the different types of "experts," and how can you become one, in a given subject-matter you want to focus on?

1. **Research Expert** - you research and interview people and subject matter, and you report on it or offer a synthesized version of your findings.

   Napoleon Hill used this strategy for *Think and Grow Rich*. He interviewed rich people like Andrew Carnegie and his other wealthy friends. From those interviews, he distilled the lessons into best practices and into useful chunks of information that helped "regular" folks understand the topic.

Oprah Winfrey is a similar example. You may know her today as one of the richest and most powerful women in the world, but how did she attain that status? By association, and the process of interviewing famous experts and people of influence on her show.

2. **Results Expert** - to position yourself as this type of expert, you merely have to have accomplished some fundamental tasks or achievements in your life. You created those results. You could merely sit down and list all the things you have learned and experienced in life or business, and if you could help other people create similar results in a shorter period of time, or help them to avoid the challenge you had.

   Then you're the "been there, done that" type of expert. You can say, here's what I did, and here's how you can do it better, faster, whatever.

3. **Role Model** - this type of expert positioning happens all the time to people who are often in the public eye who have earned a good reputation.

   I interviewed a friend of mine Ben Wilson, for another book of mine called, *Big Money With Your Book... Without Selling A Single Copy*. Ben was one of the results-experts I used to showcase the results you could create making money with your book. In fact, if you get the book, you'll learn that he made $53,000 in 45 days, just from selling an $8 e-course.

   Anyways, Ben told me in our interview that he got a phone call from someone he'd never met before, who offered him

$20,000 to go spend the day with him and help him with his business.

Want to know the best part?

Want know the business Ben is in? And what his book is about? Ben's book is called, *Hotdogs Saved My Life*. Ben's in the hot-dog-expert-concession-stand-business. *(This totally cracks me up…hotdogs!!!)*

Back to Terrie.

Now, instead of pretending to be something she's not, or having more experience than she has to manufacture her authority positioning, I suggested that Terrie "interview" the top people in her field, and turn those series of interviews into her book.

Inspired with new clarity, Terrie went out and did just that. What she found, was a very warm reception, from the people she respected most in the industry, so Terrie followed the exact steps of our system. After she got the clarity she needed, Terrie "set a date" to promote the pre-launch of her book.

What she also did, was coordinate her referrals, and the energy and momentum of having just connected with the greatest thought-leaders in her industry, and Terrie created a significant amount of buzz during her the pre-launch of her book *If You Knew Their Thoughts: How An Animal Communicator Can Transform Your Relationship With Your Pet.*

How did things go for Terrie?

"Within 60 days of my pre-launch, I gained 30 new clients in initial consultations totaling $4,500. The Epic Author Mentorship helped me to drive my book to international #1 bestseller [and] that helped me establish my credibility and expand my reach. By properly marketing and celebrating the stages of my book, it pole vaulted the sales of my business."
—Terrie Matz

As an Animal Communicator, Terrie works with animals that have all types of challenges:

- Adjusting to changes in their environment (families moving or going on vacation)

- Urination control

- Stress when someone leaves or someone new approaches

- Being spiteful or mean

She also provides Animal Reiki Services, which helps animals experiencing stress due to: illness; surgery, pre and post; transitioning to a new home; family going on vacation without them; another animal in the family that's left the home or holding onto past experiences.

What do you need to pre-launch?

You only need three things in place.

Seriously, you're not going to believe how simple this is.

I call this the 3 D's:

1. Design the cover
2. Describe the book
3. Set a Date

You can do this.

Design The Cover

Once you have a title and subtitle, get your design done.

Ideally, you settle on a design that you really love, but you do have the option to change it, so you could upload a "good enough" cover and always make it better later.

In fact, my wife pre-launched her first book with a different title and cover than the final draft. Her original title was, *How to Overcome Your Money Issues in 10 Easy Steps*. After doing a bit of keyword research, (which will help people find your book more easily), Robyn decided to change the title, so of course, the cover had to change as well.

The new title became *Mind Over Money Management: Strategies Your Financial Advisor Won't Give You*. And she even added a super long subtitle with a ton of keywords to increase visibility.

The truth is, it was hard for Robyn to make that change, but had she not pre-launched the book when she did, she would have left a ton of money on the table. In the end, it's hard for her to even remember the old book title, because she's so happy with the new one.

Nobody ever complained, even mentioned the fact that her book title changed.

Don't let "perfect" get in the way of "possible."

Describe The Book

Another requirement for a pre-launch through KDP is a description of the book. This is SOOOOOOO simple.

All you really need (besides basic contact info) is to fill in these blanks:

(Why not just do it now? It doesn't have to be perfect. Just come up with a placeholder and you can make it better later.)

Title: _____

Subtitle: _____

Description of your book: _____

_____

_____

The description could be something short and sweet, or you can write a description that can be repurposed on your author central page (on KDP), or it could be the content on the back of your book.

Category selection is included in the uploading process as well, which I will go over below.

Set A Date:

Setting a date is sometimes the hardest part because then you are actually giving yourself a deadline and have to get your book done.

Tony Robbins said, "If you talk about it, it's a dream. If you envision it, it's possible, but if you schedule it, it's real."

This definitely makes it real. In fact, so real, that once you pre-launch your book on KDP, you have exactly 90 days before your book is delivered to your customers who pre-ordered it…so there's a fire under your ass to get it done!

Once you set a date, work backward to choose your pre-launch date. Make sure you give yourself extra time, though. Because once you have your final draft of your book, you will still need it to be edited (which could take two weeks or so) and you will need it formatted for the Kindle version as well, (which could also take a week or two, depending).

More Advanced Strategies Prior To The Pre-Launch

If you want to implement more advanced strategies before your pre-launch to make it even more successful and impactful, here are a few things to consider. This is something we cover in my Epic Author program, but it's a bit in-depth, so I'll just touch upon it now, so you understand all your options.

The "pre" pre-launch process consists of:

- Target Market Research
- Search Engine Research
- Advertising Research
- Competitive Analysis
- Book Title Creation (Using Keywords)
- Book Outline (More in-depth Table of Contents)
- Engagement with Your Circle of Influence
- Advertising and Marketing

<u>Amazon: Choosing Categories</u>

Your choice in categories can actually determine whether or not you become a best-selling author, so if that's important to you (which I think it should be), then you must be strategic when choosing your categories.

This strategy is a bit complex, which is why I recommend hiring a publishing team that can do it for you. If you are serious about becoming a #1 Bestseller, you can learn our step-by-step process in our Epic Author Academy and Mentoring Programs, so you'll be able to do it yourself. Or, as a client, you also get exclusive access to our team who can do it for you at our "family" rate.

ACTION STEP

1. Set a date to launch your book: _____
   (work backwards to pick your pre-launch date).

2. Describe your book:

Title: _____

Subtitle: _____

Description of your book:

_____

_____

_____

3. Design Your Cover:

Who will you hire to design your book? _____

ELEVEN
7 Phases Of Your Epic Book Launch

"I wanted books to change me, and I wanted to write books that would change others."
—**Jack Gantos**

In 2015, I co-authored *Your Epic Book Launch* with 20 other bestselling authors who were using their books to build 6 and 7-figure business.

The premise of the entire book was based on the marketing or "launch" of the 7 different types of books that you can publish. Each of these, we described as being a different phase of your publishing process.

Each is an opportunity for you to celebrate, and market, your same content, packaged slightly differently to the world. It is truly a phenomenal marketing strategy, and one that I use every day, with every one of my books, and all of my clients.

What I'd like to do for you here, is go into a little detail about what each of these 7 phases are and how you can use them. (See Figure 3.)

NOTE: You can choose to do these in any order. There is no right or wrong way to promote your books—*except for not promot-*

ing them.

What I suggest you do, is consider which of these 7 phases, or different formats of your book, you want to have, and then schedule each new "launch" approximately 1-3 months apart. If you do this, the content you create for one book can easily dominate your marketing for the next 12-24 months.

Your book is your most powerful marketing tool.

(Note: Some of what I share with you below is modeled after content we printed in *Your Epic Book Launch.*)

Declaration

The "declaration" phase of your book promotion simply means that you tell the world about your book. Share it everywhere. Celebrate all of the stages of your book creation, starting with the decision to write your book. But this extends to engaging your audience and getting their feedback on titles and covers and content, etc. You can also "interview" people for your book, and this is another opportunity to create interest and buzz for your book.

But better yet, if you do this properly you can leverage this into getting more clients, more speaking engagements, free publicity, and media attention. (I discussed this in detail in Chapter 3.)

Pre-Launch

We already covered this in some depth in Chapter 10. But in short, a pre-launch is an arbitrary day that you choose to promote your

Figure 3

book and make it available for pre-sale. I suggest this strategy to help you drive as many sales as possible, at as low a price as possible (often $.99), so you can achieve a #1 bestselling book before your book is even written. Immediately, you can start to use your new bestseller status in your marketing to drive more interest and buzz about your upcoming book.

This is done using Kindle Direct Publishing and Amazon.

<u>E-Launch</u>

<u>Why Every Book Needs an E-Launch:</u>

This is the day your book actually goes live. If it doesn't, you don't have a book for sale. Given that your book is going live, why not make an event out of it and promote the fact that it is going live? Your customers will receive their copy of the ebook version of your book on their Kindle app automatically, the next time they log-in. This is also a great opportunity to tap your initial readers for the oh-so-important reviews you're going to want to have for your book.

<u>Understanding the E-Launch Process:</u>

An E-Launch is so much more than just your book being available to your customers. Yes, that is a great feat to have accomplished, but the goal is to have an EPIC launch, and that means you must maximize this day for all it's worth. This is another opportunity for you to engage your readers, get them to actually read your book, and also to leave you reviews. That why the E in E-Launch stands for Engage. Your job is to engage and entice them to take action. The Launch process actually starts well in advance of your book going live. Planning is the key to having a successful E-Launch, since you've only got one day when your book goes live for the first time. So, make it count!

How to Transition From a Pre-Launch to an E-Launch:

There are a few things you will need to double check, and a few others you will need to put into action as you transition from a Pre-Launch to an E-Launch. As you come up to your E-Launch day, you want to make sure the final ebook file you upload to Amazon is ready to go. This means your editing, formatting, links, images, and everything else are also ready. Amazon requires that you upload the final version of your book and change from draft to final version settings within KDP 10 days before your launch day.

Here is how to plan for this:

If your launch day is the 12th of June, the exact time your book will be delivered is 12am Eastern on the 12th (9pm Pacific on the 11th). Then you have to count backward 10 days from there exactly to know your cutoff upload time. In this case, it would be 12am Eastern on the 2nd of June (9pm pacific on the 1st). It's not exactly straightforward, but Amazon will send you emails reminding you of your cutoff. To be safe, make sure you upload about a day before this cutoff. Once you've uploaded your book and changed it over to the final version, you will have a small grace period of a week to make changes that are absolutely necessary. Your cutoff for these changes is three days before launch; in this example, it would be 12am Eastern on the 9th of June (9pm Pacific on the 8th). **This is a hard deadline.** Amazon will gray out your account, and you can't make any other changes once you reach this deadline. Whatever they have will go out to everyone who pre-purchased your book, and even if you make an update to your book at a later date, most customers don't have their accounts set up to receive those updates. That is why it is so important to get the right version out to them initially. If there are mistakes and you are asking for reviews, you could have some major issues on your hands because people will leave bad reviews for bad editing and formatting more than anything else.

<u>In preparation for your launch day:</u>

- In advance of "the day" you've already reached out to your list, contacts, friends, family, clients, social media friends, promotional partners, your launch team, and anybody and everyone you can find, so they have an advance copy of your book in their hands. This is so they have already read it and have a review ready and waiting to post on launch day.

- You've got engaging videos setup for your launch day so you can post, message, and email them throughout the day to encourage and remind people to leave their reviews.

- When you notice a new review posted, shoot a quick video thanking that person and send it to them. (You should also post this on social media.)

- Ideally, you have already been doing a massive Facebook ad campaign to promote your upcoming book, and you have new ads scheduled to promote and retarget your previously mentioned group of people for your special day.

- You have press releases which have already been deployed to boost your book page rankings in and around the day your book goes live.

- You use a Virtual Book Tour to talk about your book and

appear on as many podcasts, TV and radio shows and blog posts as possible. Ideally, you'll have many of these recorded in advance, so you will have to work with the presenters and website owners to get them to help you out by making them live on your E-Launch day.

- Since you are most likely using our bonus in your book, you must have those bonuses ready to deploy, and those website pages built to capture their email and deliver the bonuses.

WARNING ABOUT REVIEWS: In advance of your E-Launch it's nice to send a PDF version of your book to your "launch team" to get feedback and prepare them to leave a review of your book as soon as it comes out. The challenge is that Amazon tracks if you've purchased the book, opened the book, and reviewed the file, to confirm that you've completely read the book.

These elements determine if a review will "stay up" on their site or if Amazon will "remove" them. The key here is to make sure that your reviewers know this in advance. You will want to guide them through the process, of how to leave a great review that Amazon will love because just reading the PDF version of your book isn't enough.

Amazon also doesn't like it if it appears the reviewer knows the author, so you have to be *very specific* with the people leaving reviews for you to not talk about any personal relationship with you. Whatever you do, DO NOT buy reviews. These are guaranteed to get taken down and potentially sabotage other valid and verified reviews that you've received. Paid reviews are a waste of your time and money

ACTION STEP

I've created a PDF you can send to your reviewers, along with your book, that will help walk them through the process. You can get the PDF now at: TrevorCrane.com/amazonreviews

Free Launch

There are 2 types of free launches we'll cover here. One is using Amazon's exclusive 90-day promotion, and the second is using a Free + Shipping promotion strategy, outside of Amazon.

Why Every Book Needs a Free Launch

"Why would anyone ever want to give away their book?" Because your book is bait, it's not the main course. One of my mentors, Russell Brunson, earned over 10 Million Dollars giving his book away for free. And he's not the only one. (This was using the Free + Shipping strategy.)

Understanding the Free Launch Process On Amazon

In order to do this type of promo on in Amazon, you have to make your Kindle book exclusive to Amazon for 90 days. This means it can't be live on iBooks or any other site that Amazon doesn't own. If your book is on iBooks already and you want to deploy this launch strategy, you can turn off your iBooks version for those 90 days, and you will be fine.

Free Launch Strategy Using Kindle Select

There have been very recent changes in how Amazon handles this strategy when using Kindle Select.

Previously, authors were paid for the sales they made during the days their book wasn't free in the 90-day period. They have decided to make a new policy that says they will only pay you based on the amount a reader reads.

<u>Free + Shipping</u>

Many thought leaders have seen the long-term value of big readership of their books. So much so, that it is a major strategy in most of their marketing.

This means every icon you can imagine including Tony Robbins. The strategy is pretty basic. They get the paperback for free, and all they have to cover is shipping. (Average $6.95 or $9.95.)

If the thought of figuring out this process and websites and funnels and credit cards and shipping, etc. seems too complicated, I'll offer you our most effective and profitable book funnels that you can use, when you're in our Epic Author Academy and Mentoring programs.

(This is a pretty handsome perk of being in the program.)

<u>Paperback Launch</u>

Again, this is pretty straight forward. When you are planning your Paperback Launch, you first need to choose which company will print your book.

Each company has different guidelines for their printing process, so you want to get this out of the way before you finalize your cover and formatting. The two big names in the print-on-demand space are CreateSpace and IngramSpark.

We have used both, and they each have their plusses and minuses, so it's up to you. CreateSpace makes it relatively easy to get your book printed and up on Amazon for purchase in a timely manner. It's also easy to make changes to your book if there is an error or you want to adjust your content.

It's also slightly cheaper than IngramSpark, but there can be a slight bit of a quality cost.

The printing can sometimes mess up and is not always perfectly aligned. There can be folds on the spine that mess with your cover design.

If you're concerned about quality control then as much as CreateSpace is an incredible resource, you might choose IngramSpark instead. (Also, CreateSpace issues you a free ISBN number, which is nice, and saves you a bit of time and money.)

If you want your book to look it's best, and have that traditional publisher quality, or to get your book in bookstores, then you should consider IngramSpark.

The downside is that if you need to make changes to your book, they will charge you each time.

It really forces you to make sure that your editing and formatting is absolutely handled before you upload your book to them. They also charge a little bit more for printing, and IngramSpark offers hardcover books, which CreateSpace does not.

There are many other companies who print books, and they are growing and changing all the time.

Many require you to purchase a huge amount before getting price breaks, but that is only good if you want to order a ton of copies. It kinda defeats the print-on-demand awesomeness that Ingram and CreateSpace offer you.

If you want to do specialty printing, you many need to look elsewhere.

Do your research before choosing a printing company and weigh your options.

I used Bookbaby for a couple of hardcover books I wanted made for two of my daughter's books: *The 3 Ninja Kitties*, and *Kitty Wars*.

Podcast Launch

Creating a podcast around your book is a really great strategy for many authors. I helped one of my clients become the #1 podcast in its genre, and its fans are rabid, and growing. Check out, Cult-ClassicHorror.com to see all the "gory" details.

The nice thing about a podcast, is that you get to connect with a whole new group of people who like to get their content via audio or video, instead of print. Again, it's also just using the same content you already have in your book. Or, you can choose to interview people around your subject matter and magnify your reach.

Audiobook Launch

An audiobook is the spoken version of your book. You most likely knew that, but did you know that without one, you are alienating almost half of your target audience? Yep, that's right. We all have different modalities we like to use to consume information. **Also, there is typically much more money per sale with an audiobook.**

Now that you've decided that you need an Audiobook Launch, it's time to make it happen and maximize your efforts.

The place where you will be uploading your audiobook is on

the website www.acx.com. This is the best place to upload your audiobook because it will distribute your audiobook to Amazon, iTunes, and Audible. It's the site used by some of the top authors in the world.

Hardcover Launch

A hardcover version of your book is the Holy Grail of book formats. It holds the most perceived value among authors, publishers, and book sales. A hardcover book tends to be more durable than other versions, and they look great on bookshelves.

By the time you are ready to start the Hardcover Launch of your book, it has probably gone through many edits and revisions.

Your ebook and paperback versions of your book don't cost that much to change, so it's probably been pretty painless for you to make continual improvements.

This means that you have the best version of your book ready for hardcover release. This is a good thing because it is the most prestigious format of your book.

Just Take One Step At A Time

Tough it may seem like a lot, you can do this.

At first, when you start trying to roll a big rock, it doesn't feel like it's going anywhere.

But after a while it will gain momentum, and start moving faster and faster.

Same thing with your book.

You just have to get started.

ACTION STEP

1. Plan about 1-3 months (or more between each of your book "launches") and you should have a powerful marketing message to share with the world for the next 12-24 months.

   _____

   _____

   _____

2. Decide now, which are the first 3 types of launches you want to use, and in what order.

   _____

   _____

   _____

PROFIT

"The first step is to say that you can."
—**Will Smith**

TWELVE
Promotion With A Launch Team

"Building a team: Individual commitment to a group effort—that is what makes a team work, a company work, a society work, a civilization work."
—Vince Lombardi

I'm pretty excited to include this chapter in the book.

Why?

Because, while I've known about book launch teams, I've never really used one…until recently. And this is cool, powerful, and excellent.

Now first, I'm guessing you've recognized the emphasis I've been putting on not going it alone in this entire book. Well, nothing is more important than building a <u>great team</u> to help you create momentum around your marketing.

In case the idea of "marketing" may *scare* you, rest assure that it is not that complicated. All marketing really is, is communication with other people.

That's it.

In this chapter, however, let's focus on how you can use a *launch team* to help you communicate and reach more people, sell more books, and get more book reviews…which of course can lead to you getting more clients or furthering your cause.

What Is a Launch Team?

It's a small group of people who you hand-pick to help you spread the word about your book when it comes out. They are eager and willing to help you promote your book. This means they are going to give their time, ideas, skills, and access to their networks to help ensure your book launch is a success. *How cool is that?!*

A good launch team can help you multiply your reach, and relieve some stress, so you don't have all the responsibility on your shoulders.

Let me show you the power of this.

Meet Pat

Okay, "reacquaint" yourself with Pat Petrini. (I introduced you to Pat in Chapter 1.)

Pat is the #1 bestselling co-author of the book *The Miracle Morning for Network Marketers,* and a past client of mine who is absolutely killing it with his book.

Pat is an entrepreneur in the REAL ESTATE industry but got his start in direct sales and network marketing, where he was known as a TOP producer and consultant.

Recently, I interviewed Pat for another book of mine called, *Big Money With Your Book …Without Selling A Single Copy!* During that interview, something really stood out that I wanted to mention here.

Pat, very successfully used a book launch team to promote his book.

If you want to super-charge the launch of your book, you might want to model what Pat shared with me about having a pre-launch team.

Originally, Pat's goal was to get a team of 100 people who would agree to help promote the initial launch of his book.

In order to attract and incentivize this launch team, Pat and Hal Elrod, Pat's co-author and partner, offered their friends, family, and followers numerous bonuses that created excitement and anticipation for the upcoming book.

They also gave them an advance look at the book, and connected them to a private Facebook group, to help build momentum and excitement for their upcoming book.

In the end, their pre-launch team grew to over 900 people. This team agreed to:

1. Buy the book,

2. Talk about and promote it, and

3. Leave a review on Amazon.

This is how Pat puts it:

> *"As far as the launch goes, we did this pre-launch team. We offered a bunch of access to all the free bonus content, early access to that. We gave people a free digital version of the book for being in the pre-launch team…*
>
> *We made the book available on Amazon on a certain day but at the lowest price we could possibly list it so that anybody in the*

pre-launch team could get access to the physical book as well at the lowest possible price…

Our goal was to have a hundred people in the book launch team and after we had told people that it was closing, but if they wanted to invite their friends, we ballooned up to 900 people in our pre-launch team. That was 900 people that had made a commitment to buy the book at the cheapest possible price, and get all the free stuff that went along with it, but also to leave a review.

We tried to layer on if there's anything we could give to people to be a part of that team and we created a little Facebook group. We started promoting it, getting people to become part of that team, and then we did a, 'Hey, there's a few days left to be a partner of the book launch team. If you want to invite any of your friends, then now's the time. Here's the deadline…'

Right off the bat, we had a good launch strategy, and we got a bunch of people rallied behind the launch of the book and people that were committed…

The book has grown in sales pretty much every month, maybe with one exception, but pretty much it's grown in sales every single month since it launched for the last year plus."

The Fortune Is in the Follow-Up

Pat also said that only about one-third of the people who agreed to participate in the launch actually followed through and left reviews on Amazon.

He also acknowledged that this did not happen by accident.

One of the most powerful things he did, was to personally connect with and privately message every single person on this list.

> *"About a third of those people actually left reviews.* ***I followed up with everybody.*** *I'm pretty good with follow up and pretty persistent. I had a list of every single person that committed. I was sending emails, following up with everybody that had left a review. I think if you want to really have the best launch possible, you've got to be willing to put in that kind of time to do that stuff."*

One of the things I love about Pat is that he's not afraid to do the work.

In this case, his "work" was to show his growing audience that he CARED about each and every one of them.

That's a nice strategy to model.

Who makes up your launch team?

The first group of people you probably want to approach, are the types of people who you think would be interested in your book. As I'm suggesting in this book, you should have a very clear picture of WHO you're writing the book for.

With that as a start, I suggest you try to find as many people like that as possible and ask them if they'd like to be part of your launch team.

But you should also consider anyone and everyone you've ever connected with. Quite simply, you never know if someone you know would be a good candidate if you don't ask.

In my first book, *High Paying Clients*, I talk about how the first and best place to look for high-paying clients is in your own "Pond." This simply means they are people you know or are connected to.

According to an article in *The New York Times*, the average American knows approximately 600 people.

They might be your friends or family, or on your email list; or maybe you're friends on Facebook, or connected on LinkedIn, or Twitter, or Pinterest, or any other of the million places online.

Or, they could be people you know at work, or at church, or at a local networking group that you know of, or they could be on about one hundred other places offline.

Now, I want you to see the possible POWER of a good launch team. Consider who "they" know. In my book, I call these, "Other Ponds." These are the people who hang out in the circles, groups, and connections that your contacts and connections share. This means they are just one degree away from you. Just a phone call, an email, or an introduction away.

Well, if the average American knows approximately 600 people, and you were to do some simple math, your reach into Other Ponds is 600 people X 600 people = 360,000 people.

Not a bad sized pond.

What Are the Benefits of a Launch Team?

Well, among other things, a launch team, will allow you to capitalize on a marketing tactic called "one to many." Here's what they can do:

- Leverage their social media following to your book.
- Leave positive book reviews on Amazon.
- Download your book from Amazon, even if you've given

them a free copy of the book ahead of time. (This is very important since you want "verified" reviews from Amazon.)
- Make referrals to other influencers and people they think will like your book.
- Contact the media for you, book you speaking gigs or interviews on podcasts, blogs, radio shows, schools, businesses, with business leaders, educators, community service leaders, local clubs, local politicians, churches, mosques, synagogues, non-profit organizations, local sports teams, or clubs, etc.
- Engage on your Facebook page to create excitement and buzz.
- Make t-shirts, hats, mugs, or magnets.
- Write articles about your book; make short videos about it, and post it online
- Establish a Goodreads page about you and your book

Why would people join your launch team?

People will join your launch team for many different reasons.

Some will join just to do you a favor. Others will be raving fans of you and your work. Others, couldn't really give a hoot because they just joined to get the bonuses you provide. Regardless of their reasons, it's important for you to address them where THEY ARE.

Remember that they are giving of their time and energy and hard work and focus and they loved you enough to support you and the launch of your book.

Many people will be there, simply because they like to help other people. They like to belong and be a part of something, and they like the feeling of accomplishment and significance, and it's up to you to nurture that.

When the message of your book connects with the right people, they will consider it a privilege and a pleasure to be part of your team and spread the word.

One more thing about the "who" here… One quality, committed team member is more valuable to you and your launch than an ocean full of undependable people.

What can you say, to recruit your launch team?

Well, recently I just started my first book launch team, for my book, *Big Money With Your Book,* so I can share some of the scripts I've been using when I'm chatting up people on Facebook.

I certainly didn't do everything right, but so far, I think it's going pretty well. In about a week, I have 100+ people on my launch team, and so far, I've gotten 25 book reviews.

Go to TrevorCrane.com/booklaunchteam to find some scripts and conversations that might give you some guidance about what to say, and what you can use to coordinate your own launch team.

Here are some other tips that might help you with your launch team:

1. Choose how big you want your launch team. (Quality is better than quantity—and recruit cool people for your team.)
2. Offer some cool bonuses as incentives for them to join.
3. Have an application with 3-5 questions—so they are more likely to take it seriously.

4. Create a FB group page and a welcome video/post.

5. Communicate regularly, and try to add fun, interesting and engaging posts.

6. Ask them questions, and get their feedback.

7. Choose the launch team's assignments and weekly tasks, like reading a copy of the book (or chapters) and providing feedback, reaching out to relevant bloggers and influencers who can promote the book on their social media and forums, downloading the book on launch day (to get your Amazon excitement building) and writing reviews on launch day.

8. Utilize your team's talents help improve your sales copy for a one-sheet, or your website; enables you to check for formatting errors, make graphics for social media, and create promotional videos to help spread the message with influencers.

9. Have fun and don't forget to thank your team!

ACTION STEP

1. Plan about 1-3 months (or more) between each of your book "launches" and you should have a powerful marketing message to share with the world for the next 12-24 months.

   _____
   _____
   _____

2. Decide now, which are the first 3 types of launches you want to have, and in what order.

   _____
   _____
   _____

3. Make a plan for your own Book Launch Team.
   - How big do you want your launch team? (Quality is better than quantity—so recruit cool people for your team.) _____
   - What cool bonuses could you offer as incentives for people to join? _____
   - What 3-5 questions could you ask people so the "qualify" to be in your book launch team, so they are more likely to take it seriously?
     a. _____
     b. _____
     c. _____

THIRTEEN
Big Money With Your Book

> *"Money is not everything but it ranks right up there with oxygen."*
> **—Zig Ziglar**

In this chapter, I'm going to cover this subject briefly, because I've already written another book, that goes into much more detail.

It's called, *Big Money With Your Book ... Without Selling A Single Copy*

If you'd like a free copy, I'll gladly send you one for free, all you have to do is pay for shipping. TrevorCrane.com/bigmoney

Beyond Your Book

It's important to understand that your book is only the beginning.

Most authors have difficulty seeing beyond just getting the book done. But your book is the platform upon which you could and should build your authority, credibility, celebrity, and expertise.

In order to do this, however, you must have products and services to sell, and in this section, we will discuss some of the quickest and easiest options.

The worst way to make money with your book is by selling it.

The real profit from your book will come from the sale of your products and services, not from the sales of your book.

The average US non-fiction book sells about 250 copies a year and around 3,000 copies over its lifetime.

Consider your book an invitation into your business. Your book is better than any other marketing tool you'll ever have.

Think about it, your prospects live behind closed doors, and they do everything they can to keep them shut. The world is trying to get their attention, and they don't have time to be distracted by the riffraff.

They get bombarded with sales messages in their email, on their phone, on their Facebook page, on their LinkedIn profile. They read them in their newspaper, see them on TV, hear them on the radio, see it staring back at them on their cereal box in the morning. Your prospects are doing everything they can to delete and reduce the noise and clutter.

Essentially, your potential customers are perpetually trying to <u>ignore</u> your messages and invitations.

To get in the front door, you need them to choose to let you in.

To get them to take your call, you've got to get them to DECIDE to give up their precious time just speak with… *"Who are you, again?"*

Unless you convince them to opt-in to your email list, or go out of their way to visit your business, or take your call, selling anything to them is nearly impossible.

Enter your awesome book.

When it comes to getting a successful person's attention or a busy CEO's attention, few things compare to sending a potential client a professionally published book along with a well-written letter. Suddenly, you have no competition. Suddenly, you're not a sales person with a pitch.

Instead, you're an authority and an expert on a particular subject. Thanks to your book, your prospect has opened their doors.

<u>There are only three ways to make more money in your business:</u>

1. More Clients (you find new people you can help).

2. More Money (you sell more or higher and products and services).

3. More Frequency (your clients buy more often).

Now, for some people, talking about making money is exciting. For others, it can be a scary concept.

If you're one of those people, you might think, *Oh no! I don't want to sell anything. I don't have to sell, do I? Can't I just write my book? I mean, if I write my book, then won't people just magically show up and give me their money?"*

Sorry to disappoint you, but in a word:

No.

If you're going to build a business and really earn some income, then you're going to have to sell something. The good news for you is that it's actually much easier than you might think. The following is a list of some of the products and services that you can probably add to your current business without too much trouble. (See Figure 4).

Remember this…

You can have all the knowledge, all the wisdom, and all the expertise in the world, but if you don't have sellable and scalable products and/or services, *you're dead in the water.*

So, let's make sure at the outset you strategically plan to create some products and programs that you can offer.

Recurring Revenue Is Your Goal

Here's the question, "What can you sell once, and what will allow you to continue to get paid, over and over and over and over?"

What can you offer that creates recurring revenue that will allow you to fulfill your purpose, expand your mission, and make a difference? And how can you do so in an easy, systematic, and predictable way that you can enjoy? And that people will love?

What Are You Going To Sell?

How are you going to make your difference? Here's a list of your options or vehicles that you can use (i.e., your products and services and programs.)

1. Audio Programs
2. Books (ebooks, Audiobooks, Paperback, and Hardcover)
3. Coaching and Consulting (one-on-one and/or group coaching)
4. Online Courses and Programs
5. Partnerships and Joint Ventures
6. Masterminds
7. Membership Programs
8. Seminars/Live Events
9. Software
10. Speeches/Keynotes
11. Tele-seminars
12. Video Programs and DVDs
13. Webcasts and Webinars

THIRTEEN - BIG MONEY WITH YOUR BOOK

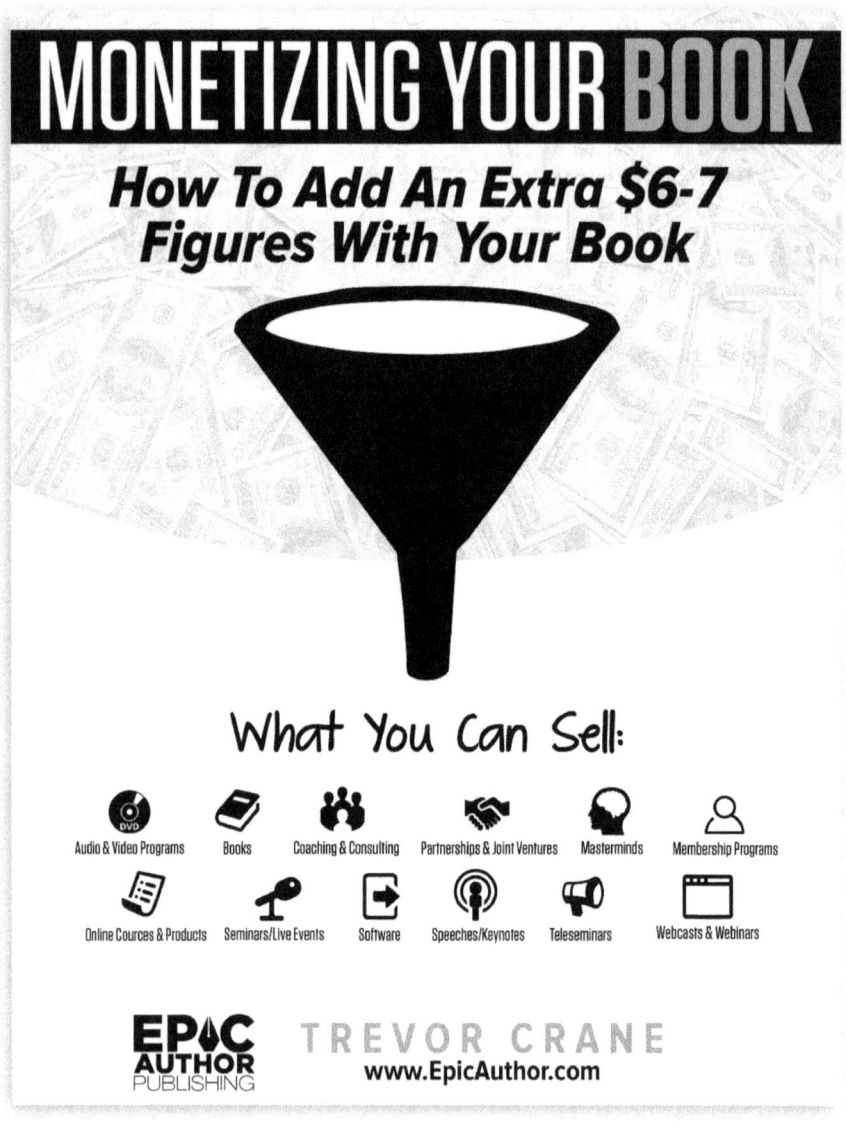

Figure 4

Here's Some "Show Me The Money" Math

These are four options from the list above that you could use to build a healthy 6 to 7-figure business.

EARNING DISCLAIMER "FINE PRINT"

I'm not even remotely implying that everyone (or anyone) will earn 6 to 7 figures, or any amount of money at all, as a result of reading this book, or attending one of our webinars (or any other training for that matter).

I have absolutely NO CLUE what you'll earn if anything. I don't know you, what you know, or what you're willing to do (or not do), and we will not insult your intelligence by implying otherwise. Again—I'm sharing this with you for purposes of clarification, and I am in NO WAY implying you'll make any money. In fact, I guarantee that if you don't take action, you won't make a dime.

*However, if you are cool and coachable and committed, and willing to do whatever it takes, the following examples should empower you and give you a clear path as to how you could make money **if you were to follow through**.*

Clear? Cool.

Coaching and Consulting

For this example, let's say you charge a very reasonable and average monthly coaching fee of $1,000 per client per month. Let's say that you have 25 clients.

Here's the money math:

$1,000 X 25 clients X 12 months = $300,000

Monthly Membership

For this example, let's say you charge a very average monthly membership fee of $50 per client per month, and that you have 400 clients.

Here's the math:

$50 X 400 clients X 12 months = $240,000

Online Course or Product

For this example, let's say you charge a very reasonable fee of $550 for your course, and you sell 40 per month.

Here's the math:

$550 X 40 clients X 12 months = $264,000

Mastermind Group and Retreats

For this example, let's say you charge a typical fee of $36,000 for your mastermind, and you sell 12 per year.

Here's the math:

$36,000 X 12 people = $432,000

Total:

$300,000 + 240,000 + $264,000 + $432,000 = $1,236,000

Adjust these numbers to find out what would be most appropriate for you and your business. **You must feel congruent around your offer, or you'll have a hard time selling them to anyone.**

Do these numbers sound unrealistic?

I'm guessing that they do. But they have merely been provided for demonstration purposes.

While you might not know how to sell all, or even any, of those items, the question is, "Which of those most appeal to you?"

The reality is, there are plenty of people out there making a million dollars or more per year doing just <u>one</u> of these things. My suggestion is to pick one that suits you best and focus on it.

Simplicity is your friend.

Your Time Is Now.

People have a greater need than ever for your message, your book, your guidance, mentoring, coaching, and your products and programs.

At the end of your life, one of the ways you evaluate how you've lived is whether or not you've helped other people, and whether or not you made a difference to other people's lives.

Why not make that your career?

I look forward to helping you along the way.

For support and free training go to: TrevorCrane.com

ACTION STEP

1. What are you going to sell on the backend of your book?

_____

_____

_____

2. How much will you charge for each product or service?

_____

_____

_____

3. How many of each would you like to sell?

_____

_____

_____

4. What's the total amount of money you would like to make?

_____

_____

_____

THE END?
This Is Only The Beginning

"If I can do it, you can teach a cat to do it."
—**Trevor Crane**

Congratulations for making it to the final chapter.

I can't wait to read *your* book.

In fact,

I can't wait to write the *foreword* of your book.

(Assuming that is, that you write an excellent book.)

At a minimum, let's connect on social media. I want to personally celebrate your success along the way and be part of your exciting journey.

Assuming you have been taking this book seriously (and seeing that you're still reading, it seems like an accurate assumption), I'm sure you recognize this is certainly not the end.

Instead, this is the beginning of creating your ideal life, impacting more people, and stepping into your greatness.

It may take a lot of soul searching, strategic planning, and work, but it will all be well worth it.

You have definitely not reached the end.

This is only the beginning.

THE "END"

BIG MONEY PROGRAMS

1 - FREE TRAINING TO BECOME AN AUTHOR

Make this the year you "finally" write your book!

Becoming a published is the most powerful way to grow your business, your brand, your mission and your legacy.
—Trevor Crane

FREE TRAINING
EpicAuthor.com/free

11 - EPIC AUTHOR ACADEMY

This is my life-changing online course which is a 3-part program designed to walk you step-by-step with everything you need to get your book done, and how to use it to SELL your products and services ...*without stopping what you're currently doing or wasting time.*

- WRITE a great book – faster than you ever dreamed possible
- MARKET it a #1 bestseller guaranteed – plus a 12 month promotion plan
- MONETIZE it and add an extra 6-7 figures to your business

BONUSES Include:

- 3 Core Money Making Funnels to help you drive targeted traffic into an automated system that help you create "Goodwill" and "Increased Revenue"
- 2 Free Tickets to Epic Author Summit – LIVE EVENT

EpicAuthor.com/academy

III - EPIC AUTHOR MENTORING

This is a 6-month journey we will take together to transform your book, your business and your life. (Perfect for business owners, authors, speakers, coaches, consultants, and entrepreneurs.)

All we do is create bestsellers and build the big businesses behind them.

During this incredible 6-month life-changing program, you'll receive:

Epic Author Academy plus:

- Personal Project Manager
- Decade In A Day
- Voxer Access To Trevor 24 Hours A Day
- BBB Mentoring Team
- Become A Featured Case Study
- Duplicate Our Most Profitable Marketing Funnels
- BONUS #1: VIP Tickets to our 3-Day Live Event
- BONUS #2: Mastermind and Networking

EpicAuthor.com/mentoring

*Results described in this book are not typical.

I AM IN NOW WAY MAKING PROMISES THAT "YOU" WILL CREATE SIMILAR RESULTS.

Most people are not willing to follow through. Most people won't do what it takes. Most people would rather make excuses, than create results. I don't know you, your business, your skills, strengths, weaknesses, opportunities or limitations. For all I know you'll do nothing with this information. What I do know, is that it's possible.

The rest is up to you.

ABOUT THE AUTHOR

*"A mentor is someone who allows you
to see the hope inside yourself."*
—**Oprah Winfrey**

I struggled for over 20 years to write my first book. I'm not proud of it. But it's true. I had ideas for books and spent time journaling, and doing research for different book ideas. I wasted years.

But for one reason or another, I just couldn't get a book done.

Fast forward to today. I'm a 10-time #1 international bestselling author. I spend my days helping people build their ideal business, so they can live their ideal life. I help them publish and profit from their books and share their message and their mission with the world.

My team and I specialize in creating products and programs that help entrepreneurs create phenomenal business success. In 2014 alone, my team and I **helped our clients generate *more than* 3 million dollars in <u>bottom-line</u> profits.**

"Profit" is <u>what's left</u> after you pay all your expenses. It's what you <u>take home</u> and buy bacon with. Or veggie-burgers…whatever you're into. Oh well, I guess after Uncle Sam takes his cut. So, it's after *THAT*… but it's money in "your" pocket.

I feel very fortunate to have been blessed to help make a *difference* in people's lives worldwide. That's the most important thing to me in the world—that, and my family and my friends. That's what matters to me most.

But having this type of abundance <u>wasn't</u> the norm for me. It's taken a lifetime of work, monumental mistakes, and trial, error, success, failure, setbacks, and so forth…

I was born the son of a horseshoer in Phoenix, Arizona.

Growing up, my family struggled to put food on the table and pay the bills. Our family slogan seemed to be "We can't afford it." My parents fought about money a lot. We didn't have extra money to buy nice things. We didn't take vacations.

Then, when I was seven years old, just after my great, great grandfather had passed away, I found out that, *at one point,* our family had *millions* of dollars.

With a growling stomach, I looked around me and wondered where all that money had gone.

I found out that subsequent generations had *blown* all the money. Hearing the story, I decided then and there that I would figure out how to make millions and rebuild the family fortune. That's been a goal of mine, ever since.

But it wasn't all sunshine and rainbows. I found myself building up some success, only to lose everything—*twice.*

The most painful experience was when I filed a 2.2-million-dollar bankruptcy in 2009.

The most painful part was losing my 2-year-old daughter. Her mom left me; took her and left the state.

I sold everything in my house that wasn't bolted down and even sold some things that were. I dug up plants and trees from around my yard and sold those—I sold EVERYTHING.

At possibly my lowest low point, I gave away my dog, Mojo, to a friend, because I didn't have a place to live.

Fortunately, I had friends who let me stay with them. I moved from basement to attic, and from couch to couch.

One of the hardest parts of it all was the feeling that no one would ever trust me again, because I was convinced that I was…

A Loser

In that state, it felt as though I was the last person in the world anyone would ever want to take advice from. Let alone, did I think I could ever be an author. *Why would anyone ever want to read one of my books?* I wouldn't wish "losing everything" on my worst enemy.

I made a series of poor decisions. Then worse ones.

I refused to accept the help and mentoring of others. I was stubborn. I thought I knew it all, but inside I knew I was a fraud. And I kept thinking that I "should be" smart enough to figure it all out by myself.

I blamed others for my problems. I started fights. I sued the people who had "wronged" me. All of this without really looking in the mirror and facing the truth. Staring back at me was the guy *ultimately responsible* for where I ended up.

But finally, I started getting it right.

I stopped blaming others. I accepted that "I" had actually been the <u>cause</u> of all of my problems. The great thing about that was, while I couldn't control other people, I could take charge of myself.

Over several years, I rebuilt my business and my life.

I sought out new mentors. I found the fortitude to push through challenges, and better yet, I got insight from people who cared about me and were smarter than I was, so I could avoid problems in the first place.

Yet, while it worked. It still wasn't great.

I was very busy putting in a lot of effort for little return. **But, when I finally became an author, everything changed.**

Instantly, my positioning shifted. The <u>trust</u> and <u>authority</u> I was trying to **PUSH** down peoples' throats, was now nearly automatic. I stopped having to work hard to convince people to work with me.

Instead, people were *attracted* to me. They wanted to work with me.

But I want to be clear; it wasn't "only" my book.

It was *everything*.

It was everything I'd gone through. It was my mindset, the mentoring, and the MAPs (Massive Action Plans) that my new circle of influence gave me.

But, here's also what I found:

The problems and pain are part of the process.

Our Setbacks Are Setups for Success.

Today, my life is as about as abundant as life can be.

I'm happily married to the woman of my dreams, *Robyn*. I get to spend an incredible amount of time with my beautiful daughter, *Phoenix*. It's important that we play, and have fun, and travel, and have adventures.

Little Miss Phoenix Rose Crane, is a 9-year-old, 9-time bestselling author. She also starred in a movie she wrote called *Kitty Wars*. My daughter co-founded Super Kids Books Publishing with me and is on a mission to help 1000 kids become Super Kids' book authors.

I'm more proud of my daughter and her accomplishments than anything I've ever created.

Today, instead of struggling to get by, we give back, and we volunteer our time and donate to the charities we love most.

I don't share this to brag. I'm just proud of the life we have and, quite honestly, I cherish it, because it wasn't always this way.

No one who succeeds at anything great does it alone.

I believe you need the right mentoring, mindset, and the right MAP to succeed.

But also, it can be as easy as changing the "music" you're listening to.

Ever get a song stuck in your head?

Maybe you hum it all day. Maybe you hear it when you go to sleep at night. Maybe you made the colossal mistake of going to Disneyland and getting on the ride whose tune follows you around for days, *"It's a small world after all…"*

This is similar to the inner-monologue that goes on in our heads. It talks to us about our abilities and our expectations.

But when you change the music, when you choose to tune into *different* **input**, you start to focus on things differently, and you get *different* **output**.

If you aren't getting the results you want, maybe all you need to listen to is a new tune.

I hope this book has been the right tune for you.

More Books By Trevor Crane

TrevorCrane.com/books

ACKNOWLEDGEMENTS

"Storytelling is the most powerful way to put ideas into the world."
—Robert McKee

I cannot even begin to express how grateful I am for all of the people who came into my life exactly when I needed them most. Your life-changing wisdom and belief in me supported me when I didn't believe in myself.

Thanks to my wife, Robyn Crane for tolerating me even when I make incredibly stupid decisions, like publishing 10 books in 90 days. Thanks to my daughter for being soooo awesome—*because five of those books were yours.* You are so sweet and so talented, and we are the luckiest parents in the world to have you in our lives.

Thanks to Ashley Peterson, who my wife describes as being "our everything." Without you, we would have only a fraction of our success. (And it wouldn't be nearly as fun.)

Thanks to Jon Low, and our entire publishing team here at Epic Author Publishing. You helped me get things out of my head, and heart, and onto paper, so that it could change people's lives.

Thanks to all of my teachers and mentors, and the people who

ACKNOWLEDGEMENTS

have blazed the trail ahead for me and everyone else in the world. (Including: Mike Koenigs, Ed Rush, Chandler Bolt, Rob Kosberg, Jack Canfield, Mark Victor Hansen, Robert Kiyosaki, Tim Ferris, Seth Godin, Grant Cardone, and so many more.)

Thanks to Tony Robbins. You helped brainwash me, when I was in desperate need of a bath. Everything changed for me, for the better. While you hardly know me, you've been a close friend to me. You've always been there to give me great advice (through your products and programs) and when I speak with you out loud to myself like a crazy person. (I have conversations with you, where I speak both sides of the conversation out loud. *You give great advice by the way.*) And, you chair the head of my imaginary CIA Round Table that I keep in my head. (CIA = my Central Intelligence Agency.)

Thanks to all the authors I love. You are too numerous to list specifically here. But you inspire me. You entertain me. And I couldn't imagine living without your books.

Thanks to you, the reader. I write my books for you.

I hope you use this one to change the world.

TrevorCrane.com/freetraining

www.ingramcontent.com/pod-product-compliance
Lightning Source LLC
Chambersburg PA
CBHW050200230526
45470CB00001B/171